Cinderella's Still Going to the Ball

Cinderella's Still Going to the Ball: The Untold Story of Abuse, Rescue and Rehab

---

Dr. Shaunte' McFarland, M. Ed.

McFarland Ministries
2015

First Printing: 2014

ISBN 978-1-312-67252-9

Library of Congress Control Number: 2014960314

McFarland Ministries
P.O. Box 349000 #109
Kailua, HI 96734
www.shauntemcfarland.com

This book recounts events in the life of Dr. Shaunte' McFarland according to the author's recollection and perspective. While all the stories are true, in some instances names of individuals and places have been changed. Some identifying characteristics and details such as physical properties, occupations and places of residence may have been changed in order to maintain the anonymity of those involved.

Ordering Information:
Special discounts are available on quantity purchases by corporations, associations, educators, and others. For details, contact the publisher at the above listed address.
U.S. trade bookstores and wholesalers: Please contact McFarland Ministries
Tel: (213) 293-5352 or email drshaunte@shauntemcfarland.com

Dedication

To the Alpha, my King, my Lord, my Savior , the Omega, the One in whom I live, move and have my being. You gave this book to me and now I return it unto you. My prayer is that your anointing falls on all that open its pages and are blessed according to your riches and glory.

Contents

Acknowledgements

I would like to thank my husband, Christopher McFarland, Sr. for his unconditional love, faithfulness and selflessness. Thank you for your listening ear and honest critique. You have truly cherished me, realizing that I was your helpmeet, your good thing, rewarded when you found favor of our Lord.

To my son, Christopher McFarland, Jr., you are very precious to me. I take great responsibility and pride in your care. God blessed us with you and charged us with teaching you His word. I hope that one day you will understand what great heights I went to, in order to see you succeed in this cruel world as a talented and gifted African-American man.

To my family, thank you for your loving support through the years. Know that I have been blessed through the good and the bad. The Son shined through the rain and made beautiful rainbows as a promise of his unfailing love for us.

To Mrs. Jean Austin, you didn't know how much you influenced me when I was your student. I am now a certified educator and like you I take out the time to help reach my students' needs.

To my sister, my first best friend, thank you for your love and patience. I thank God for you and our relationship.

Preface

"There is no greater agony than bearing an untold story inside you." - Maya Angelou

In 2008, God spoke to me, "You're going to minister to women". Immediately after service I sought out the first lady of the church I was attending. I needed her guidance and grooming. I believed it was no one better to model myself after than her. I assumed that God meant, one day I was going to be the first lady of a church and head the women's ministry.

For years to come I would be frustrated with life as I did not serve in any women's ministries. Instead I would work only in children's ministries writing Sunday School curriculum, spend my Saturday nights cleaning the church and teaching home Bible studies in the local community.

When I wasn't completing my duties at the church I was at home being purged and stripped of all the hurt, pain and darkness I still carried within. God had done an amazing work in me. In fact, He is still doing a work in me and has promised to "carry it on to completion until the day of Christ Jesus".

Transparency carries an undeniable power to encourage soul searching and inspiration for greater. The memoir you are about to read is tremendously transparent and written with the hope that it will aide you in your "happily ever after".

Introduction

Water running forcefully into the tub and tears streaming from my cheeks meeting the water in an emotional tributary; as the scrubber spits emerald green grass stains and sun kissed dirt from the summer onto my face, I am completely overwhelmed. Out of the five or so pairs of tennis shoes from my male cousins, I managed to find a pair that was only two sizes off. It must have been the pair from my Aunt's youngest son. He's only a year younger than me.

This is how I spent my night before the first day of my 8th grade year; vigorously scrubbing hand-me-down tennis shoes that my cousins used to mow the yard all summer. I wasn't crying because they were boys' shoes. I was actually happy and excited about them. They were my first pair of name brand shoes. I finally had my very on pair of FILA's. Be it as it may, I was crying because I felt perpetually trapped. It seemed to be no end to the pit that I was undeniably tumbling deeper and deeper into.

It seemed all was lost. I had nothing and I never did. How was I ever going to get out of this situation? Not even a glimmer of hope existed in me. The "normal" lives of others were such an illustrious mystery to me. Girls at school would speak about their trips to the beauty salon with their mothers, adventures to the mall and viewing new movies at the theatre. All of which I had never done, seen or knew existed. Their talks sparked an undying fire inside of me to one day escape and experience for myself.

I had no wicked stepmother or stepsisters but at this place, by default, I am Cinderella. I am talented, beautiful and deserving, yet I am trapped in a cellar with no one to keep me company but my dreams. The word "Cinderella" has, by analogy, come to mean one whose attributes were unrecognized, or one who unexpectedly achieves recognition or success after a period of obscurity and neglect.

This is the story of my rescue; an exhaustive account of how I overcame abuse, neglect, poverty, loneliness, isolation and beheld the fruition of my happily ever after.

Cinderella’s Still Going to the Ball

Chapter 1: Once Upon a Time…In a Far Away Land

Once upon a time, there was a man who had a lovely and beautiful lady as his wife. They had one daughter only and her name was Cinderella, who was very dutiful to her parents.

I've always loved the tapping sound of "church shoes". The musical melody always felt so regal. My imaginary queenship becoming more and more alive as the sound of each foot harmoniously tapped against the mosaic tile floor. If only I had known that those taps were unknowingly signaling the "Taps" to be played at the funeral procession of my innocence; I might have requested a shoe of a softer bottom. Perhaps, I could have gone out in silence. Maybe then, I wouldn't have this line of demarcation. For the rest of my life those tiny, patent leather, baby shoes would be a reminder as the beginning of my end.

As Mama and I sat in the Greyhound bus station awaiting our fresh start, she opened her wallet and pulled out a crisp wallet-sized photo. "This is Jerry. He's going to be your new Daddy," Mama said. "But what happened to my old Daddy?" I questioned. "He's still your Daddy, but now you have two Daddies." Two Daddies?! I must be the luckiest girl on Earth. She gave me the picture to hold while we waited. I looked down at my pink and white ruffled socks and shiny shoes dangling above the floor. Until Mama yelled, "Jerry!" I didn't run to him because she did. I ran because I was so excited to receive my new gift, another Dad. I saddled my tush on his foot, wrapped my legs and arms around his massive calves and melted into his warmth. I wrapped myself around his leg so tightly. He just robotically escorted us to his truck with this beaming toddler yelling "Jerry, Jerry!" the entire way home.

The drive to our new home was the longest and most peculiar sight I had ever witnessed. "Welcome to Pine Bluff Population: 56,600," a sign read as we passed through a town vastly different from the high rises of Cleveland, Ohio, my birthplace. Honking horns, smiling faces and waving hands from the people around us, seemed to be normality as we drove through the city. Jerry even had a conversation with one man while we waited at a stoplight.

"Hey, Jerry."

"Hey, Rick."

"This is my fiancé Crystal and her daughter Shaunte'. I just picked 'em up from the Greyhound. They comin' from Cleveland," Jerry said.

"Oh, you got you a city girl? Well, ya'll have a good one."

As we continued our journey, the scenery took a drastic change. "Ya'll ever seen this before," Jerry said. "What is it?" I asked. For miles and miles all I could see were fields full of cotton. I had never seen cotton growing from a plant before; to see so much of it at one time was quite overwhelming. A fear struck me as I looked unto the never-ending horizon of cotton. *We are going to the middle of nowhere.* I thought to myself. And if the cotton fields weren't enough, we exited unto a long and winding dirt road to confirm my mental note. Finally, we arrived at "the little house on the plantation". Here we stood at a little, butter cream home on cinder blocks finished with a ruffled tin foil roof.

I was scared out of my mind. Obviously Mama was too. A huge bumblebee flew past her head and she screamed and ran a good half a mile down the dirt road. "Crystal get back here," Jerry yelled. "If you don't bother it, it won't bother you." A bumble be flying around boasting its' intimidation with every buzz and flutter was the last thing I needed.

After the coast was clear Mama came back and we dashed into that ol' shack like thieves in the night, a sticky and muggy night. The heat sweltering inside was even worse than the mayhem that had just occurred in the front yard. For a slight moment, I had grown accustomed to the new climate of the south. But I had soon found out that, "down here in these parts", it can be hotter inside than it is outside. Especially, when the only hint of relief comes from a medal box fan that sits in the kitchen window.

I looked around the room surveying my new home. Immediately to my left stood "Big Black". A cast iron, potbelly stove sitting on a throne of bricks, with a large metal pipe that ran from it's back through the roof of the home. The floor was made of dark, unpolished wooden flanks. The walls looked like they may have been peach at first, but years of punishment from Big Black had left it tainted an awful dirty brown. The furniture was also made of wood. The arms of the coach and chair were large and looked hand made. But what was mounted in front of me struck the fear of God in me. Hanging on a single nail on the mantle of a bedroom door was a distressed leather, white belt. There were several other belts that hung from the bedroom door, but this belt stood out. Not because it was white, but because of the carmine and dirt stains. This belt looks old and worn but not due to over wearing. I stood their frozen, immediately made aware of its purpose.

"Hey!" Jerry exclaimed as he elicited my fear-potentiated startle. "You don't have to worry about that, as long as you do what your told."

"He's just joking, Shaunte," Mama explained.

We continued our brief tour of the two-bedroom house where he showed us the bathroom, kitchen and our bedroom. The bedroom was large and dark with a door at the back that led to the front porch.

"This is our room and this is JJ your new brother," Jerry said. "Ya'll play in this room and this room only. But be careful on this floor. You don't want to get a splinter."

There were two beds: a metal queen bed for Mama and Jerry and a twin bed for me and Jerry, Jr. As Jerry continued to lay down the rules for the family bedroom, we heard the screen door slam and work boots march to the kitchen.

"Jerry!" the man said.

"We're back here. Crystal, Shaunte' this is my dad Elder Todd. Everybody call him Elder."

"Hi." I responded nervously. By the looks of it, Elder had a long, full day of work. Arkansas, red dirt covered the front of his plaid shirt and kneecaps of his faded Lee jeans. He was a man of few words. After his introduction he just nodded and went into the kitchen to pour himself a glass of water. After I heard the melody of the leather belts over the bedroom door I realized that that was his room and that white belt belonged to him. My mission from that day forward was to avoid the wrath of that white belt by any means necessary.

Shortly after, Mama married Jerry and attempted to enroll me into the local elementary school. My birthday is in November so I had to wait an entire year before I could start. At this point I would be starting school with JJ who was a year younger than me. I hated that. I wanted to start school so bad. I have always had a fondness for school, not just learning but also the institution of school: the principal, teacher, students, schoolhouse and the playground. There's just something about these elements that excite me.

That year of waiting Mama did an amazing thing. She did the one thing that would set me up for greatness: homeschool. Mama taught me colors, numbers, shapes and how to read with the help of the phenomenon that is Hooked on Phonics®. When I arrived to Kindergarten the next year I was several levels above my peers. Most of whom could not read or write yet. I was utterly bored and as a result I began to cultivate a gift that would bless and annoy: excessive talking. No matter where a teacher would place me in class I would just talk and talk and talk.

Needless to say I was not the class favorite. I started to be shunned by not only my teacher, but also my classmates. I can remember my Kindergarten teacher, Mrs. Martin, leaving a stack of heavy books in the time out corner. Whenever my talking became overwhelming, I would spend my days in the dunce corner staring at the wall and holding books until I got my act together.

I finally gained a little respect back from my classmates at the class' Valentine's Day party. Finally, a day had come for food, fun and most exciting for me—socializing. After we enjoyed our treats, the teacher let us know that if we cleaned our area quickly we would get a surprise at the door. Of course we all frantically cleaned our areas, grabbed our belongings and at the teacher's "ok" headed to the exit.

There were mothers present passing out candies. We opened our bags as we left and each mom gave a smile and a treat. The assembly line continued and to my surprise, standing at the end was Jerry. I looked up to him and with all of my innocent energy yelled, "Thanks Daddy!" I had never called Jerry "Daddy", but I didn't want the other kids to think any less of me than they already did. He just smiled back and said, "You're welcome, baby."

Yes! Jerry hadn't ruined it for me by exposing the truth. This was when I began to wear a "mask" and appreciate its value. People will treat me according to what they know and I had the power to manipulate their treatment to some extent. But this covering would not only cover me from the harsh treatment of others. It would also conceal the identity of those causing me harm.

I remember watching a movie about dreams a few years ago. The characters had the power to go into another person's dream and extract information. They were frankly called "extractors", people who performed corporate espionage using experimental technology to infiltrate the subconscious of their targets and extract information through shared dreaming. During one scene the leader was speaking to an intern about dreams—

COBB: Our dreams reel real while we're in them. It's only when we wake up we realize things were strange,

Ariadne gestures around them-

ARIADNE: But all the textures of real life- the stone, the fabric…cars...people... your mind can't create all this.

COBB: It does. Every time you dream. Let me ask you a question: You never remember the beginning of your dreams, do you? You just turn up in the middle of what's going on.

ARIADNE: I guess.

COBB: So... how did we end up at this restaurant?

ARIADNE: We came here from...

Ariadne trails off, confused.

COBB: How did we get here? Where are we?

Ariadne THINKS, unable to remember. A FAINT RUMBLE begins.

ARIADNE: Oh my God. We're dreaming.

Cobb nods. The RUMBLE is BUILDING.

COBB: Stay calm. We're actually asleep in the workshop. This is your first lesson in shared dreaming, remember?

Ariadne looks around, mind REELING. Cobb BRACES. The restaurant VIOLENTLY EXPLODING AND IMPLODING PARTICLES OF FURNITURE, WALLS, PEOPLE FLYING AROUND.

Ariadne WONDERS at the MAYHEM WHIRLING around them- Cobb SHIELDS his
head against the debris. She sees him-

ARIADNE: (shouting over noise) If it's just a dream, why are you covering your…

Ariadne is WIPED FROM HER SEAT BY A MASSIVE BLAST (Nolan, "Inception", 2010)

This is the way that abuse begins in a person's life: like a dream. You have no idea how it began. You are locked in without any way out. Lest, you are awakened and snapped back into reality.

Chapter 2: After A Time…Negated and Tainted

But while she was still very young, her mamma died, to the grief of her husband and daughter. After a time, the little girl's papa married another lady. This lady was evil and haughty, and had two daughters as disagreeable as her; so the poor girl found everything at home changed for the worse.

There aren't many memories a person retains from their childhood. However, the memories that remain are the most joyful and the most traumatic. Memories of birthday parties, family trips, along with painful accidents; sit in mental files opened at the most inconvenient and awkward times. Minute instruments such as smell or taste can involuntarily bring that memory to the forefront of mental projection. For me it's holidays.

"It's the most wonderful time of the year!" The radio in the local gas station blasted the perfect chorus into my ears. I love Christmas. Always have, always will. I can remember riding through the small town of Altheimer, Arkansas bright and bushy-tailed whenever the Christmas decorations were put on display. My favorite decorations were the metallic-garland lined candelabras that were placed on the rugged, wooden light posts. It had magically and pleasantly hidden the town's eyesores. It had become a winter wonderland overnight. Whenever we went into town I had to have a window seat. It was time to indulge in the city's holiday immersion of bright lights, Christmas trees and jingle bells.

The year was 1989, the last holiday of the 80's. I was sitting on the wooden floor adjacent from "Big Black" staring at our 3 ft. Christmas tree atop the living room end table. It was a small tree that most refer to as a "Charlie Brown tree," but I didn't mind one bit. The bundles of silver and red garland made it quite full. The multicolor lights pulsated in the most relaxing tempo that seemed to warm my face with every glow. I heard a knock at the door and in walked Santa Clause. Well, not the traditional Santa Clause. He was 6' 3", 180 pounds, wore a taffeta navy blue suit with black lapels, black Stacy Adams dress shoes, a golden earring with a cross that hung from a thin gold chain, a highly-moisturized box haircut—that was not quite a jerry curl but close, with his arms full of Christmas gifts. It wasn't even Christmas day yet. No. This was not the ordinary Santa Clause this was my father, James Anderson, Jr.

"Come here baby girl!!" He yelled as he dropped the gifts by the end table holding up our Christmas tree. I ran to my father with all the energy within me. I smiled so hard that my cheeks ached. "Here, open up your gifts," he said. I looked to my mother for approval and she nodded. I dove into my gifts wrapped in pink, my favorite color, topped with glamorous golden bows. Amidst all of the shredded gift wrapping was everything I wanted for Christmas: a new black dress with emerald green plaid around the collar, ruffled on the sleeves and tiered three levels for the skirt. A set of princess, pearl jewelry for dress-up time, a dark brown baby doll with a nightgown for her and one to match me, a new pair of black, patent leather dress shoes and white ruffled socks.

"Go try it on," my dad said. I remember feeling so beautiful and accepted. Being accepted is one of the most wonderful feelings a young girl can have. "Let's take a picture, " my father motioned as he pulled a Polaroid camera out of his luggage.

"Daddy can you take our picture," I asked Jerry.

"Daddy? That's not your daddy. Never call him Daddy, Shaunte'."

My father had spoken and let it be clear that he did not approve. He looked at my mother and I could tell by the look on his face, that he thought this title had been given to Jerry in gesture to replace him.

"Oh, ok. Mama, can you take our picture?" That was the only person's title that I was sure of. "Ok." She agreed under her breath as she rubbed the now blooming belly that carried my precious sister. With a single caress she let my father know, *I am unbothered and have moved on.*

The camera flashed and out poured the picture. "Wow, the picture comes right out." I exclaimed. "Yeah, this is a new camera, the best one out," my father gloated. "I have a surprise for you baby girl. You're spending Christmas with *your* family and me this year. We're going to Cleveland tomorrow morning. Go pack your things."

I ran to that back room without question and packed my bags. My father slept on the couch that night and we slept in the back room. I would just stare at the fire from the small furnace all night. There was no way I was going to sleep. I stayed awake until the sun rose and before I knew it we were on a bus headed to Cleveland.

It was one of the most interesting trips of my life. I spent a few days with Mama's only sibling, my Auntie. I loved spending time with her because I got to spend time with my first cousin, who I didn't realize I missed so much. I also had the chance to spend time with my father's sister and paternal grandmother. These were all welcomed visitations. The unwelcome visitations involved bars, strippers, girlfriends and running to the point of being dragged to avoid missing city transportation.

One night my father had left me in the care of one of his girlfriends. It was pretty cool because she had a nice apartment and three kids. All I saw, was a group of friends to play with to bide the time. We were having a great night. After we ate a spaghetti dinner the girlfriend took us out to the candy store. She told us if we moved quickly we could get back before it gets dark out and watch a movie. When we got to the store the sun was starting to set. She bought her daughter and I candy necklaces and bracelets. We took turns biting pieces off of each other's candy jewelry. I had never had one before. It was my first and last time having such a treat.

"Let's hurry guys, it's starting to get dark," the girlfriend said. The white streetlights were beaming like spotlights on a superstar at a concert. We started to play a little game of running through the darkness and then jump into the luminous patches. Our game came to a jarring halt when we heard hurried footsteps coming toward us. And then suddenly under the spotlight was a woman in a tattered white t-shirt, covered in blood.

"Help me!! Help me!! He's going to kill me!!"

"Who," my babysitter yelled. "My husband, he's trying to kill me!"

We started running to the apartment with the battered woman close behind. My heart and lungs felt like they would explode. As we got to the stairs of the apartment we could here the battered woman's husband scream, "Get back here!" Oh no. He's found us and from the sounds of it he's close. My father's girlfriend was trembling trying to get the key in the door and even dropped them. This is the end, I thought. She unlocked the door pushing all of the kids inside and the battered woman. She turned off all of the lights, grabbed the phone to call 911 and huddled all the children in the middle of the floor.

The battered woman was crying loudly. Still in complete terror even though she was behind a locked door. "You have to lower your voice," the girlfriend said. "If he hears you, he'll know you're in here and you're going to put me and all my babies in danger." The girlfriend called the police and as she was giving them the address the husband started banging on our front door. "Come out here now," he yelled. "Get away from here. I have the police on the phone and they will be here any second," the girlfriend exclaimed! "You called the police? If they arrest me, I'm gonna kill you."

The battered woman started to walk towards the door. "Are you crazy," the girlfriend asked in a whisper? The woman looked back with a look of defeat and uncertainty. Then, the girlfriend got an answer from the people on the other end. The receiver was loud enough that we could all hear. "Ma'am we're on our way, there are units in the area. They should be there in less than 5 minutes."

This would be a long five minutes. The man continued to bang on the door, rattling the security chain lock. We couldn't help it anymore; the violence and horror of it all had reached a boiling point. I started to cry and scream in terror, as did the rest of the children. They started to yell, "Mommy! Mommy!" Surely, she could put an end to this. But the girlfriend, like the battered woman, was helpless against the rage-full husband.

Then I saw the lights. Those trademarked red and blue lights of the police brought a comfort over my entire body. The officers ran up the stairs and grabbed the man. He yelled, "We were just having a talk. We don't need the police. She can tell you herself."

The battered woman opened the door with a newfound bravery, now that the police had arrived. "We were just talking," she said. "What," the girlfriend exclaimed! "You put me and my children in danger. Saying that he was going to kill you. Look at you. You're beaten and covered in blood!" "I'm sorry," the woman said. "I shouldn't have gotten you involved." *Great now I won't sleep right for a week.* That lady just ruined our perfect night.

The next day my father took to my Auntie's house to spend one last night with her before I went back home. "Your mom had the baby," she said as I walked in. "Oh wow, I can't wait to see her," I said. My father interjected, uninterested in hearing about any baby. "Well, I'll be here first thing in the morning. See you tomorrow baby girl."

My cousin Pookie ran up and hugged me around the neck. It felt so good to have some normalcy. Like all children, I had to tell someone about what happened the night before. So I told my Auntie what happened and I got an unexpected, paradigm-shifting, response.

"I'm sorry you had to go through that Shaunte'. This is always happening to you."

"To me?"

"Yeah, witnessing all of this violence. James couldn't keep his hands to his self either. That's why Crystal divorced his *cuss*."

I started to think and try to remember those moments. I remember the arguing, but for the life of me I can't remember the physical violence. Either way I believe it and I would never look at my father the same. My heart broke for my mother and myself. Our happy home had been ripped apart. As far as I was concerned we were banished to Arkansas. I didn't understand. Why Arkansas? It was the middle of nowhere. We were a lot poorer and a lot more miserable. But surprisingly, after hearing this news, I was ready to go home, back to the slow and miserable life in Arkansas.

When I got back home the Christmas decorations were still up. Honestly, I was done with Christmas this year. I was kind of ready for it to be over. There were just too many awful events that had taken place during the supposed, "most wonderful time of the year".

But then, Mama walked around the corner with a glowing bundle of joy in her arms. She had on a navy blue and white onesie with white bows throughout her thick, curly red hair. She was beautiful. She was about five shades lighter than me and had the brightest green eyes I had ever seen. I expected this, but not. My mom had hazel eyes and was a little lighter than me. Jerry was mixed and had green eyes and red hair. This baby looked like my mom, but had Jerry's hair and eye color. So even though we didn't look alike, I knew she was my sister and I would love her to the ends of the Earth.

"Do you want to hold Maxine?" *Maxine was such a beautiful name for such a beautiful baby.* "Yes, Ma'am." She had the sweetest smell and grin. She was heavier than I perceived. My little 5 year-old arms could barely hold her up without Mama's help. I instantly fell in love with this little baby. She was so sweet and precious in my arms.

School was starting the next week. I couldn't wait. Our first assignment was to write about our Christmas Vacation. There was no way I was going to tell them what really happened on my break. I couldn't tell them I had another daddy, a "real daddy" or about what happened in Cleveland. So I just told them what I wanted them to know. I got a lot of gifts and I have a new sister.

That night I was exhausted and uncomfortable. I just wanted to get a good night's rest. How soon I had forgotten that we all slept in the same room: JJ and me in the twin bed, my newborn sister in the bassinet, Mama and Jerry in the queen bed.

We had a large bedroom, however. It even had a fireplace in the center of the back wall. The fire was comforting at times. The light from the flames helped ward off my fear of the dark and the crackling of the wood would sometimes lull me to sleep.

Unfortunately, JJ and I had the loudest twin bed this side of the Mississippi. Every time you moved the springs would squeak. It was relentlessly uncomfortable. When we first went to bed, JJ and I were tossing and turning. Moments later Mama and Jerry came to bed. I kept trying to get comfortable, squirming from one side to the other.

"Stop moving in that bed and go to sleep," Mama yelled. "But I can't get comfortable."

Lord, why in the world did I talk back? Mama got out the bed and walked over to me. I was scared and mesmerized. My mom had on a beautiful satin teddy with lace trim. *What does she have on?* I thought. While I was wondering Mama was whacking. "Stop moving and go to sleep"

Nothing puts you to sleep quicker then a good whooping. Well I learned today: DO NOT TALK BACK.

While I was sleeping I was awaken by the strangest noise but based on the lesson I learned earlier tonight I didn't dare move to investigate. My eyes began to focus and in the light of the fire I witnessed things that are hard to say. I was so confused, is Jerry hurting Mama like James did. Why isn't she running? Does she need help? Why isn't she asking for help? Is Jerry going to try to hurt me like that too? I shut my eyes instinctively but the moaning continued. I wanted to put my hands over my ears but if I moved they would know that I was awake and another whooping would be sure to follow. I concluded that this whooping would be far worse than the first one. I had violated their privacy by being awake. I saw something I wasn't supposed to. I heard things I wasn't supposed to. What am I going to say? *Ya'll woke me up, so it's not my fault.*

If I had stayed asleep I would have never known what had happened. I had no choice but to lie there and wait for it to be over. Once I heard Jerry snoring I felt all was clear. I looked down to my feet and there was JJ's eyes trained on mine. He was awake too.

It seemed we would have to play this "I'm awake but I'm asleep game" every night until the day we moved out of that house. I tried really hard to fall asleep before Mama and Jerry would come to bed. And sometimes I would, but like clockwork I would be wakened by the awkwardness of Mama and Jerry. Sometimes JJ would tap my foot to see if I was awake too. Sometimes I would tap back in a way of saying *"Yeah I hear it."* Sometimes I would pretend to be asleep. I hated that JJ touched me. I didn't want anyone to touch me while "that" was happening. It was a painful time for me. My chest and head would ache whenever I hear them "doing it". Sometimes I thought that I would start to bleed from my eyes and ears.

Chapter 3: The King's Son Held a Ball …Welcome to Stank City

But she bore all her troubles with patience and grace, not even complaining to her father, and, in spite of her hard toil, she grew lovelier in face and figure every year. Now the King's son held a grand ball, and all persons of quality were invited to it. Including the two stepsisters..

Have you ever wished you had a soundtrack that played as you entered a room or maybe a band to play a score at your most dramatic moments? I have. The day Mama told me that we were moving to "New Town", I wish I could have had a choir dressed in gold and royal blue robes to sing behind me as I praise dance to "Oh, Happy Day". I can just imagine it now…

[Mom walks into the room holding my baby sister on her hip]

Mom: We're moving to "New Town" next week.

[With a look of excitement.]
Mini Me (to pop-up, congregation): Praise the Lord everybody!

Congregation: Praise the Lord.

Me: I said…PRAISE THE LORD EVERYBODY!!!

Congregation: Praise the Lord!!!

Mini Me: Well, we have finally reached our goal in the building fund and will be moving to our new residence in "New Town". Now, I don't know where "New Town" is. But it's a whole lot better than where we are now. Ain't God faithful! Tomorrow is a Happy Day. Choir. Come on and bless us in song.

Solo: Oh Happy Day…
Choir: Oh Happy Day…
Solo: Oh Happy Day…
Choir: Oh Happy Day…
Solo: When Jesus washed.
Choir: When Jesus washed.
Solo: Oh when he washed
Choir: When Jesus washed.
Solo: He washed my sins away.
Choir: Oh Happy Day…

Mini Me: Hit it!!

Mass: He taught me HOOOOWWW To WAALLLKKK, fight and pray!! Fight and pray!!!!

"Uh, Shaunte' do you hear me talking to you," mother interrupts. "Yes ma'am."

Wow. I thought. *New Town. I can't wait to get to New Town. We're gonna get our own rooms in a big new house.* I could barely sleep the night before moving day. Boxes were piled up in our room making it look a lot smaller than usual.

On moving day, I clutched my Raggedy Anne doll as we loaded into the truck and journeyed to our new home. We drove a few miles, crossed the railroad track and made a right. A right I wondered? Why are we making a right? We continued to drive for a few miles. Then the truck slowed down and made another sharp right. Finally it stopped at a house that was smaller than our old house. I fought my emotions to make sure my look of disappointment did not show.

Mama and Jerry seemed to be happy about finally having a house of their own. We walked up the raggedy wooden steps to a kitchen no bigger than a bathroom. That's when I got nervous, if the kitchen is this small what about the bedrooms? To our left was the living room and down the short hall divided by one wall were two bedrooms. They were small but that didn't matter. We were no longer sharing a bedroom.

"I'm putting the kids in the living room. It's more space," Jerry said. "The second bedroom can be the den"

We ended up sharing a room anyway. But at least it wasn't in the same room with Mama and Jerry. They set up a bunk bed for JJ and I in the living room. I slept on the top since I was the oldest and taller than JJ. At the foot of the bottom bunk was my navy blue footlocker. It was the only thing that reminded me of being back home in Cleveland.

Mama had another baby, Joseline. She looked just like Maxine. I almost thought they were twins. In fact, everyone did. They had the same red hair, same green eyes and the cutest freckles on their nose and cheeks. Well their hair isn't the traditional red. It was kind of a coppery red. Whenever they were outside and the sunlight reflected off of them, they looked brazen. My sisters are so beautiful. Every chance I got to spend with them I would love to smell their faces and necks. It was such a magical scent and their skin was so soft. I just loved those babies. Everyone did. What's not to love?

Jerry started working for a country club in a city called Pine Bluff. He came home one day and told Mama that they were hiring maids. Maids? I thought. Mama's gonna be a maid? Weeks later she came home in a black dress with a fancy white, waist apron.

I hated that Mama worked. I was so used to her being at home with us and teaching me school. And she always worked late. The deal was sweetened a little bit when she would bring home Butterfinger® candy bars.

Sometimes if they were both at work one of Jerry's cousins would baby-sit us. That was cool. We got to stay up late and watch cartoons and when the babysitter wasn't paying attention me and JJ would sneak into our parent's rooms and go through their dresser drawers. I don't know why we were so fascinated with doing so. But the sneaking and trying not to get caught was a child's adrenaline rush.

Jerry had all of these weird cartoons in his nightstand that JJ would try to get me to look at but I refused. Mama had all of her fancy nighties in her top drawer. I touched it in amazement and then snatched my hand away in disgust. The memories of the garments she wore, and what they were for, were too much for me.

Then, one day JJ tugged my shirt, "Shaunte'. Ooooh look at this!" He pointed to the naked women and men, hundreds of them. There were magazines filled with nothing but nude pictures in Mama and Jerry's bottom drawers. "Put that back just like you found it," I said. I was done looking through drawers. I don't know what we were looking for but I surely didn't expect to find this.

We ran back into the living room where our sitter was. "What were ya'll doing," she asked. "Nothing," we both answered. "Can we go outside to play?" I asked. "No, it's time for ya'll to take a nap." JJ and I headed disappointingly to our makeshift bedroom. It was so hard to take a nap with the sound of kids playing outside and the sun beaming through the kitchen windows.

"JJ you sleep?"

When he didn't answer I looked down to see my stepbrother fast asleep. *Maybe it is naptime.* I thought. So I laid on my back and stared at the ceiling waiting for a dream to take me over. Then, I started to hear someone climbing my ladder on the bunk bed. It was the babysitter.

"I'm not sleepy yet." I said trying to explain why I was still awake.

"It's ok. I can keep you company," she said.

"My bed is too small. We won't fit," I explained.

"It's ok I'll just lie on top of you," she persisted.

She was too tall to get into my bed and she couldn't stand in it like I could. So she crawled on top of me and then yanked the cover off my body and put her legs over mine. "See I told you we could fit." She was so heavy I felt like she was squeezing the air out of me.

"You're too heavy," I squealed.

"Oh let me get up a bit."

She rose up onto her elbows, staring me in the eyes. I swiftly looked away. Then she started to pull my underwear down and whispered, "Let's play house." I didn't know what playing house was and I was completely paralyzed the moment she touched my private part.

That's what Mama called it my private part. No one was supposed to ever see or touch my private part. Yet, the woman they trusted to babysit us invaded my privacy with no restraint.

I just stared at the ceiling with my arms at my side. My body was stiff as a board. I thought if I tightened my body, like my baby sisters' do when they don't want to be picked up, that she would get the point, but she didn't. She kept tugging at me and tugging at me. "Come on," she said. "We're playing house, it's ok".

This couldn't be ok. This is the same thing I saw Mama and Jerry doing. I did not want to do it. I kept stiffening my body. But no matter how much I tightened she was so much stronger than me. I put my legs together so tightly that she could not break through. I kept my hands flat and pressed against my body. She started to kiss my cheeks and I immediately tucked my lips inside of my mouth. The stench of her saliva made me want to vomit. She wanted me to play but I refused. I was not going to do it to her. But that didn't stop her from doing it to me.

I stared into the ceiling wishing and waiting for her to stop. The room became an odd gray. It looked like a thunderstorm was coming and then, the thunderclouds were in the room. The entire room looked like it was smoking. I looked down at her to see if she would stop; to see if she saw the storm clouds too. The only thing I could see was her rubbing hair onto my private part. I had never seen such a thing. I thought, *this lady is a monster! She has hair all over her body.* Finally, she raised my underwear back up, went down my ladder and watched TV in the other room. I didn't dare move.

My brother woke up soon. But I just laid there staring at the storm clouds. My parents arrived shortly after wards. They came through the kitchen door. "We're home," Jerry announced. "Shaunte' get your lazy butt out that bed and clean this room," Mama said.

I wanted to scream. I wanted to cry. I wanted to tell Mama what happened. I wanted Mama to avenge me and beat up the woman that just touched me. But when I turned my head to look at Mama she had a look on her face that said, *Get up and I mean now.* So, I gave in and climbed down from my bed. "And why are you just in your underwear? That's just nasty. Put some pants on," Mama said. There was no way I could say anything now. I was nasty. And to seal the deal the babysitter walked past me and gave me a threatening look as she received her payment and walked out of the door.

We lived in New Town for a short period of time. Jerry had to convince his cousins to move us to "the city". And I had a feeling the city would not be a stone's throw away this time. I was happy but not too happy. I could not set my self up for disappointment again.

As we drove a foul odor began to fill the car. "Eww, JJ," I hissed at my brother and covered my nose. "What, that's not me." Jerry burst into laughter. "Naw, that's the paper mill. Welcome to Stank City." This is the nickname that people gave Pine Bluff, Arkansas, with a population of 55,000; it was a huge step up from Altheimer.

Eventually, the smell went away and the scenery improved. Large grocery stores, nice gas stations and manicured lawns. The homes in our neighborhood were so nice. We made a left into a 32 unit one-level apartment complex called Kenwood Apartments. It wasn't what I was expecting but the inside of the apartment was nice and modern. We had central heating and air conditioning for the first time in my life. There was also a laundry mat.

Prior to moving here Mama and I would do the laundry using a washboard and wringer washer. After we washed the clothes we hung them up on the clothesline. I was too short to hang them but I would hold the bucket of clothespins and handed them over to Mama when she was ready.

Playing outside was a treat now. We had a playground at the apartment complex where all the kids played. JJ and I would climb trees, take turns pushing each other on the swings and making ourselves go dizzy on the merry-go-round. One day when we were playing a brother and sister approached us.

"What's your name," the sister asked.

"I'm Shaunte' and this is my brother JJ."

"JJ? Is that his real name?"

"No, it stands for Jerry, Jr."

"Oh, well I'm Natasha, everybody call me Na-Na. And this is my brother Antoine."

"Cool, ya'll wanna play with us?"

"Sure."

Na-Na was a great friend to me. When I went to my new school, L.L. Owen Elementary. She introduced me to the other kids as her best friend. I've never had a best friend. I was so happy. We would play together at recess and at home after school. I even help her with her homework. Even her mom was nice to us.

Her Mom tried to be friends with Mama but Mama wasn't having it. They were too different. Na-Na's Mom would drink, play spades and go to juke joints. Mama was the complete opposite; she didn't drink, she didn't know how to play cards and she didn't even own party clothes. There was no way Mama would go with her to any of those places.

When we moved to Pine Bluff Mama stopped working as a maid and stayed home. It was great having her home again. But, Jerry continued to work at the Country Club.

Now I couldn't wait to get home from school. We would finish our homework quickly so that we could go outside and play. JJ didn't have much homework. His Mom was on drugs when she was pregnant with him so he was born with cerebral palsy. He was mentally retarded and had to take Special Education courses at school. He was also small for his age.

Jerry said JJ was premature when he was born and it would take him a while before he "caught up" with every body else. JJ seemed pretty normal to people that didn't know him. They just thought he was short and he didn't want people to know about his condition either. I kept his secret too because I thought they would make fun of us.

One day when we went outside to play there were some new kids and Na-Na's cousins were visiting. The girls were playing double dutch and the boys were playing basketball. Na-Na was ignoring me, which was a first. JJ and I just stood there waiting to figure out if they were going to let us play with them or not. "Hey Na-Na, can I play?" "No," she responded. "Well, why not?" "Because I said so and take your SPED brother with you."

I was so hurt. She had been my friend for so long, even my best friend. I thought to myself, *she called me her best friend. So why in the world would she reject me now? It's because her cousins are here. She's pretending she doesn't know me and making fun of my brother.* That pissed me off the most.

JJ wasn't paying any attention to the situation at hand. He was just continuing his carefree life and doing cartwheels on the court. "Come on, JJ let's go," I told him. Then, as he was coming out of a cartwheel, JJ hit one of Na-Na's cousins. Na-Na immediately attacked him. So I ran over to stop the fighting and that's when Antoine started punching me in the head. I had never been punched before. It was like a blast rattled through my brain. Then I started to feel punches in my side and stomach that made it hard to breathe.

I started to fight back. I couldn't just let this kid punch me in front of all these people. I broke away from Antoine, picked JJ off of the ground and we ran home.

"That's right you better run," Na-Na yelled! Once we got home we told Mama everything that happened. That's when Mama decided to come outside with us to investigate. "What's gong on out here," she asked? "There just out here being kids. One day they're fighting and the next day they'll be back friends," Na-Na's mother said. "No JJ kicked Keisha and that's why we were fighting," Na-Na said. Na-Na's mom smacked her in the back of the head. "Don't you see grown folks talking? You stay in a child's place. Go in the house and wait for me."

I was happy to see Na-Na get smacked but was confused at her mother's response. Why would she say we were just being kids? Why didn't she tell the truth? She watched her daughter attack my brother over an accident that he apologized for. Not to mention her son who is two years older than me, attacked me before I could break it up.

Once we got home. Mama told us to not hang with them anymore. They were bad kids. I was in total agreement. But, once we got to the bus stop the next morning Na-Na and Antoine apologized so we became friends again.

We had gotten into more fights than I can count. Over the next two years we just fought and made up. The worst fight ever happened while we were waiting in the rain to catch the morning school bus. Na-Na, Antoine and their Mother came to the bus stop that day and asked me if I was talking about them. "No," I responded. "Yes you did," Antoine said, "I heard you were talking about our Mama."

Before I could deny it and ask Antoine where he got this information from, their Mother yelled. "Get her Na-Na!" Na-Na bum-rushed me to the ground. We were in a tussle as usual and I hit her back, one good one. I could never win my fights against Na-Na. I could never land a good punch. I wasn't taught how to fight. But finally, after this year of practice, I was getting the hang of it. "Bite her Na-Na, bite her!" I looked at their mother like "Are you for real? Bite me."

I crossed my arms to cover my face thinking that's where she would bite me and then I felt a lightning bolt of pain on my chest as she sank her teeth into me. The only thing I could do to get her off was to bash her in the head with my pink, ruffled umbrella. She refused to let go even while I was striking her with the umbrella. She only released me when the school bus arrived and the bus driver told her to stop. She didn't get on the bus with the rest of us; she went home with her mother and brother.

I cried the entire way to school as I sat in the seat behind the bus driver, embarrassed and ashamed. As other kids got on the bus seeing me in agony, they questioned me but the bus driver shooed them along. Once we arrived to school, I waited for all of the other children to exit. JJ came to my seat. "Come on Shaunte'. Let's go." I was the last kid to get off the bus. I wish I could have stayed there until school was out.

I went straight to my classroom. I skipped breakfast, I couldn't bare the looks on the other kids faces or their questions as to who had won the fight. I just leaned over my desk and cried. A few of the girls from school found out what happened and had sympathy for me. They told my teacher what had happened. She didn't bother me the rest of the day or questioned me; she just let me be.

Na-Na bullied me for years. The scar from her bite I still bear to this day. Most times I tried to avoid her and others I just had to push through. The worst instances were the after school fights. We would get off the bus and every time she would try to fight me. Sometimes I would stay and try to win, other times I would just run. Finally,

Mama told me that *I had better start winning those fights*. She had had enough of my cowardice.

I had met some new friends at school. Smart ones. They made it ok to be smart. They showed me how much greater it was to be confident in being intelligent. Everyday at recess we would talk about our A's and what we were looking forward to in class. Great times. I was so happy to be amongst like-minded girls. They didn't judge me because I didn't have the nicest clothes. They were my friends because I was smart, liked by the teacher and stayed out of trouble. But one day, trouble found me.

Na-Na tried to break up our friendship by embarrassing me in front of them. "Did you tell Tiffany about your SPED brother," she asked. "What are you talking about my brother is not a SPED?" "Yes he is. He rides the short bus and goes to Jenkins." "No he does not!" I felt like Peter, the way I had to keep denying JJ.

She gathered up some kids from our neighborhood and brought the mob to where my friends and me were hanging. They all started to testify how I had a retarded brother. Then I yelled. "That's not even my real brother!" "So what, he lives with you. That's *your* brother," Na-Na exclaimed!

An anger boiled in me and I ran toward Na-Na with all my might. I slammed her to the ground and started to bash her head into the pavement. Then I started to punch her in the face until it bled. I was so angry and humiliated.

I lost my good friends because I was in a fight. Teachers started to look at me with that *you should be ashamed of yourself* look. But nothing, I mean nothing could take the long awaited victory from me. I had finally slew my Goliath.

Chapter 4: Then She Began to Cry…Forsaken

One day, beautiful new dresses arrived at the house. A ball was to be held at the palace and the stepsisters were getting ready to go. Cinderella didn't even dare ask if she could go too. She knew very well what the answer would be: "You? You're staying at home to wash the dishes, scrub the floors and turn down the beds for your stepsis-

Jerry stopped working at the country club and Mama got a job as social worker. Mama was so excited to be working for the state. It was a full-time job with benefits. I hated that Mama and Jerry switched roles as far as who would work and who would stay home. But, now that Mama had a better paying job we were able to move out of Kenwood Apartments. Good-bye and good riddance.

Pine Bluff was bigger than Altheimer but it still wasn't a large city. We had lived in the Watson Chapel School District which was considered a pretty good school district to be apart of, so the further we got to our new home the more nervous I became. I would hear kids at school would compare school districts. If you were black, Pine Bluff High was the place to be, but only if your family held a certain stature. Dollarway High was considered a run down school where poorer black kids went. Watson Chapel was a mixed school but the majority of its students were white. And then, there was White Hall the name explained it all. It wasn't even a part of Pine Bluff, but students associated with the kids who went there. According to most, White Hall is Watson Chapel's rivalry and Pine Bluff High was Dollarway's rivalry. We were such isolated children there was no way I could validate this information myself.

We pulled up to our new neighborhood and my heart sank. Nervously, I asked my mother which school district we were in now. Jerry answered for her, "We're still in Chapel." That was the only positive from my vantage point. Our house looked like a doublewide trailer. It was white with black shingles, gray stairs and powder pink trim. The ugliest house I had ever seen.

There were only two other homes on our street. The house to our right was a duplex and two college students occupied the house to our left. The guys that lived in the duplex were single and older, maybe in their early twenties. They were the type of guys I was familiar with seeing in our old apartment complex. They didn't go to work in the morning. They had strange cars coming to their house every day, all day. And once the sun went down, the music grew louder and the arguments would start.

The college students kept a lower profile. I occasionally saw them during the day. Most times they would just wave and go inside. Jerry called them stuck up, know-it-alls.

I had met a friend that lived down the street, Veronica. She was so nice. She had an older brother, Nate and her family seemed to own the entire block. She had cousins everywhere. They were all pretty cool but I wasn't interested in having anymore best friends.

However as hard as I tried, I couldn't resist becoming this girl's friend. After a year I figured she was no threat. The kids in the neighborhood found JJ annoying but never to the point of bullying him. Finally, a group of cool kids.

Life outside of the house became brighter but inside our house became darker. JJ was constantly getting in trouble at school. At the junior high school kids that took special education courses would attend class in special classrooms. They were in the middle of the building and up a flight of stairs. Any kid caught going "upstairs" would be labeled a SPED for the rest of their teenage life. It was cruel and embarrassing.

JJ took classes "upstairs" and sometimes I would see

him hanging around until well after the tardy bell rang so that no one would see him take his walk of shame. Sometimes he would skip class all together.

One day I caught him when I had a pass to the restroom. "JJ, why aren't you in class?" "Because, I don't want to be up there with those other kids." "JJ it can't be that bad. You need those teachers' help" "They don't care about us. And some of those kids are just slobbing on their desk." I didn't have a response for that. I couldn't blame him for not wanting to be there.

When we got home Jerry had a belt wrapped around his hand. Whenever someone was going to get a whooping that thundercloud I saw years ago would instantly come back. "That teacher called me again," Jerry said.

No matter how much I defended my brother in the streets against bullies there was one bully I was never a match for and that was Jerry. Jerry was brutal and relentless. He would beat JJ for about an hour every time he got in trouble at school. Mostly, teachers would call home for small things about JJ. But Jerry never asked for JJ's side of the story. If he got a call, JJ got a beaten.

Sometimes I wished I could take some of those beatings for JJ. Not a week went by that he wasn't beaten. It was like clock work. We would wait for our sisters to get off of the elementary school bus, walk home together and once we got home Jerry would be standing there with a belt wrapped around his fist. My sisters and I would go to our rooms and Jerry would command JJ. "Get in here!" JJ would inch slowly towards Jerry with his right arm surrendered to the lash. JJ used this same arm each time. It was always swollen from his beatings. After Jerry got tired of reaching, he would just yank by JJ his throat, throw him to the ground and strike him all over with the belt.

A couple of times when he was hit in the face, JJ had to stay home from school. But that was worse because he would be home all day with Jerry. To this day I don't know what happened but it must have been awful. We would come home from school and JJ would just have a blank stare on his bruised and bloody face. It was horrific.

Mama would come home and say, "Well, you shouldn't have did what you did." But I knew what JJ was going through. I wanted to speak up for him. I wanted to throw my body over his and take his beatings for him. I wanted to tell those teachers what their calls were doing to JJ at home. But I was helpless and hopeless.

When JJ was getting a beating my sisters and I would go in our room, sit in the middle of the floor; cover our ears and cry until it was over. One day Jerry walked into our room and saw us crying. "Ya'll get off the floor and stop that crying before you're next. And then you'll have a reason to cry." As harsh a threat it was, it didn't stop us. We just started going into the closet to hide and if he came in we would say that we were getting our clothes ready for school the next day.

Jerry was the epitome of evil to me. I couldn't understand why he thought he could beat JJ out of retardation. JJ was prescribed several medications to treat his condition. He even took Ritalin, which stunted his already deficient growth. He seemed like a lost cause. I even went up stairs one day to see just how mean his teachers were and he wasn't lying. They were the meanest old ladies I ever met. They definitely should not have been teaching students with special needs. Their classroom was like the Twilight Zone of Watson Chapel Jr. High.

My goal was to keep a low profile as much as I could to avoid the wrath of Jerry. There weren't many clubs or organizations that we could be a part of because every time I mentioned it to my parents they would say, "No. Ain't nobody got money for that."

Finally, I found something that didn't cost money: band. Being in the school band, I was able to get a free, loaner instrument. I loved being in the band and I excelled. It was my thing. I would sit on the porch and play the trombone for all to hear. Yes: the trombone. It wasn't the typical girly instrument like the flute or the clarinet, because you had to buy a reed for those. And according to Mama, "ain't nobody got money for that."

It was a sweet time for me. That was until I entered the eighth grade. The kids around me started to change. I started to change. My wants and needs started to shift. I started to crave the attention of Mama a whole lot more than usual. I wanted to be like her. I wanted to wear make up and paint my nails like her. I wanted to talk to her about things.

My friends and other girls I went to school with would talk about going to the beauty salon with their Moms on the weekend. They would say that they could tell their mom anything. Their Moms were their best friends. I tried this out with Mama. Bravely, I went into her room one day.

This was a brave act because I hated going into their room. It was pretty disgusting to me. Not because they did you know what, in you know where, but because Jerry had the awful habit of chewing tobacco and dipping snuff. He would use an old Jack O' Lantern that my little sisters had for Halloween to collect all of his gritty and slimy tobacco spit. What's worse is he was too lazy to dump his own spit cup. He would demand one of us to dump it for him, while he sat back on the couch with his hands in his underwear. It only took two minutes for him to do this his self. I would always think *why don't you take your hands out of your draws and walk to the toilet and dump it yourself!*

Nonetheless, I walked into her room and sat at the foot of her bed. Before I could get a word out. "Stop rocking my bed," Mama yelled. "I wasn't I was just trying to talk to you." "About what, what is it now?" "Never mind."

I gave up quickly. It took all of the energy in me to come to her in the first place. I had tried several times before: in the car on the way home from the grocery store, while she was cooking dinner, early Saturday mornings during the family clean up. She was just impenetrable. I just gave up. It had been this way for years and would stay this way for years to come.

All of the siblings had a fear of Jerry, except Joseline and Maxine. They had no reason to be afraid. They were the babies of the house. And they were the only children Mama and Jerry had together. They had never felt the wrath of the belt like JJ and me. They cried so hard when JJ or myself were spanked, my parents wouldn't dare. But, my sisters avoided Jerry at all costs.

He didn't stay home much even though he stopped working. Everyday when Mama got home from work, Jerry would take a shower and "go out". Where he went remains a mystery. At first he would tell Mama he was going to Altheimer to play cards and then it just turned in to him "going out". They were not affectionate toward one another. They didn't go on dates or do anything together. He would just grab the keys and tell Mama, "I'm about to go." She would reply with a sad "ok" and go about her life. The way I figured it Mama shouldn't be disappointed because she would always be in her bedroom watching TV and Jerry would lie on the couch in the living room fondling himself.

Out of fear and abstaining from the awkwardness of Jerry's idiosyncrasies, our isolation was birthed. JJ stayed in his room doing, who knows what. He had finally had his own room so we left him alone. Plus, if Jerry wasn't home he had Mama's nagging to fill the void. He stayed in his room to avoid Mama, the same as I stayed in mine to avoid Jerry. I stayed in my room and either did homework or document dreams in my diary. My little sisters shared a room. They were only 18 months apart. Irish twins are what most people called them. They were close as twins too.

Mama loved Maxine and Joseline so much. She would always take them with her when she ran errands, painted their toenails and invited them into her room to spend time together. All of the things I wanted but never got. I tried hard to fight the idea that she loved them more because Jerry was their Dad, but nothing could stop this notion from filling my mind. Especially when she would mention how my attitude, walk and face reminded her of my *cuss* Daddy.

I couldn't get enough good grades to get Mama's attention. I couldn't stay out of trouble enough to get Mama's attention. I couldn't kiss up enough to get Mama's attention. I couldn't hate JJ enough to get Mama's attention.

A common mantra says, "A child not loved will settle for being seen." I wanted to do more than be seen. I wanted conversation, a hi or bye, a hug or even to hear the words: *I love you*. So, I did the most dramatic thing I could. I gave away my virginity. Mama thought I was stupid because I wasn't sneaky enough and she found out. But truth is I wanted her to find out. At this point in my life, any attention satisfied me, even if it was negative attention.

That was the worst mistake I had ever made. I was building myself up to be a better person, a likable and honorable person. I purposefully threw it all away, seeing that Mama's attention meant more to me. I just wanted her to take her eyes off of my sisters for a split second to realize that I still existed and that I wasn't James. I wasn't the man that had hurt her years ago. I was her daughter too and I had desperately wanted and needed her in my life.

When Mama found out she wanted to check and see if I had truly lost my virginity. So she made an appointment for me to be examined and had invited Jerry to come. There was a doctor and two resident students. The students had asked for permission to attend the examination and Mama agreed. I had no clue what was going to happen but I definitely didn't want two complete strangers present.

To make matters worst as I was being examined she had Jerry inspect my privates to "check". Mama wanted to make sure I was utterly humiliated from my choices. "When we get home I'm beating your *cuss,"* she threatened. I knew the beaten was coming, to be honest I warranted it. In my twisted mindset I wanted to get her distracted from my sisters. But what I didn't know was that her and Jerry would take turns beating me for the next week. Every day she would say the same thing. "Who else was there?" "How many times did you do it" I always gave her the one time, same person answer but she wanted more. I wasn't lying. But now I wish I had of done more. If I had known this would happen, I surely would have.

It had been six months from the incident and Mama still wasn't speaking to me. However, she had fun speaking about me. Everyday she would call her sister and say "Girl, let me tell you about that old nasty, *cuss* Shaunte." "Shaunte' did this." "Shaunte' did that." I don't remember her ever speaking of my accomplishments before but when I messed up it was widely broadcast. She wanted everyone to know what an awful person I was. It was clear that I had lost my parents trust and love forever. I lived my life engulfed in guilt, regret and insecurity.

I ate dinner in my room instead of with the rest of the family in the living room watching TV. I didn't care. I wanted to be alone. I started to hate everyone. I stapled blankets against the windows in my room so that no light could come in. I spent hours sleeping until Mama or Jerry would kick my door open and tell me to come clean the house. Some parents joke about grounding their kids for life, mine meant it.

If I had made any little mistake or didn't clean something the way they wanted me too. I would be beaten. One day I was cleaning the bathroom and Jerry left his spit cup on the sink. I started to gag. I cleaned everything in the bathroom but his cup. Afterward I went in my room and laid down for a nap. About three minutes into my nap Jerry kicked open my door. I jerked out of my sleep still half awake, my vision blurry from the nap. "What happened," I asked sleepily. "What happened? You mean what didn't happen," Jerry answered. And then I saw the belt in his hand. My vision instantly cleared and my heart began to race.

"I told you to clean the bathroom!" He yelled as he

started beating me. "I did clean it! I did clean it," I yelled. Jerry was not trying to hear anything I was saying. After about 20 more lashes Jerry grabbed me and started choking me. He picked me up by neck, slammed my head into the wall and dragged me into the bathroom. "Look at this," he said. Barely able to breathe I responded, "I don't know what you're talking about?" "My spit cup. Clean it out now and I mean right now!" I dumped the spit into toilet, sprayed the cup with 409 and brought it to him. He hit me again with the belt as I stood before him. This time the belt was not wrapped around his fist. It was elongated so that it would reach me if I tried to run. The lash cut into my collarbone and I hit the floor in agony. "Get your dramatic, black *cuss* out of here," he said.

I cried all night. I couldn't sleep. The pain was unbearable and I had nothing to soothe it. I couldn't take it anymore. I had messed up and big time. I thought I had a brilliant plan of getting Mama's attention. I thought that she would sit with me and have "the talk"; tell me how I was too smart and beautiful to do such a thing. Maybe we would develop a relationship through the whole situation. Instead, I gave her more of a reason to despise me. I gave her the gun and ammunition to kill me internally and justification to damage me externally.

The next morning I had one goal: GET AWAY FROM THIS HOUSE AND NEVER COME BACK. I could hear Mama, JJ and my sisters getting ready for school in the background. My mind was racing. I was so anxious, I had planned what I wanted to do all night. I was going to pretend to go to school but hitchhike to a bus stop and go to Cleveland. Then I thought. *No. There's no way I could do that. My Auntie's not going to take me in. She already knew of the awful things I did. Plan B: Pack enough clothes and just try to live on the streets. No. I can't do that. I'm afraid of dogs and there are too many strays out here. Plan C: Tell my school counselor and try to get adopted or put in a foster home until I graduate. I don't want to leave my sisters and JJ behind, but I think they'll manage. Maybe Jerry and Mama will take it easier on JJ since one kid was already "taken".*

Then I heard a knock at the door. "Get up and get ready," Mama said. *Ok,* I told myself, *enough thinking time to get moving.* I had been lying on my left side the entire night to avoid putting pressure on my right shoulder. I raised my right arm to move the sheet, but it was sticking to my arm. It seemed my skin was starting to thin, no longer able to bare the fierceness of my self-induced punishment. The bite of that belt pierced my flesh and left a grotesque painting in my sheets. I pulled them off slowly to avoid more damage and prepared to put my plan into action.

It was spring and everyone was starting to wear their bright clothes, flip-flops and tank tops. There was no way I could pull something like that off today. I pulled a long sleeved, button down, plaid shirt out from the winter. It was canary yellow, so it kind of fit in. Except it was already 80 degrees in Arkansas. But I would rather get the *girl it's too hot for that* look over the *girl what happened to you* look when they saw my cuts and bruises.

When I got to school I waited for first period to start and then I asked my teacher for a pass to the restroom. "You should have went before class," she said. "I know but I'm having a *lady issue.*" That was the best excuse I could come up with. Most teachers don't question a girl with a lady issue. I grabbed my backpack to make my excuse seem more realistic and went straight to the Counselor's office.

When I got to her office she was on the phone and gave me the "wait a minute" finger. It was the longest minute of my life. Finally, she turned to me with a smile. "Good mornin', what can I do for you?"

"I'm having some problems at home."

"What kind of problems?"

I couldn't put it into words so I unbuttoned the sleeve on my right arm, then the buttons on my left. I slowly pushed the sleeves up on both arms. She winced at the sight of my bruises. "Ok, roll your sleeves back down. Who did this to you?" "My stepdad." "Ok, well write your information down and go back to class. I call you up later."

I left feeling a sense of relief and nervousness. I didn't want JJ to see me at school. I had made my mind up that I had said my final goodbyes to the family this morning. I didn't want to explain anything or feel any guiltier than I already did.

It was the last 20 minutes of seventh period; the last class of the day and the counselor still hadn't called for me. Had she forgotten? Maybe she was still looking for a foster home to pick me up after school. So, I used my same excuse from earlier to go back to see her. This time she was unoccupied and had her purse on her desk. I thought maybe she's going to take me herself. "Ms. Wright, did you find a home for me? You didn't call for me, so I asked to come see you." "Oh no, I forgot to tell you. I called your stepdad. He said that he would talk to you when you got home."

I didn't bother explaining or begging. It was evident that this woman was not going to help me. Why would she call him? What was that supposed to do? I didn't say another word to her. I went to the girls' restroom after all. I just sat on the toilet with my jeans still on and just cried. There was no one I could trust. No one to help me.

When I got home Jerry was standing there with the

belt wrapped around his fist. I wanted to turn around and run, but what was the point? Jerry could see the fear and anxiety in my eyes. "Yeah Ms. Wright called me today. She told me you said your *step daddy* beat you. Well guess what I'mma beat that *cuss* again. Get over here!" At least I had on long sleeves and jeans. The belt had no access to my bare skin. Everything was a blur from that moment. I had lost all hope of life.

One day I had the chore of cleaning out my parents extra closet, separating the winter clothes from the summer clothes. Some of the clothes needed to be folded because they were just thrown inside. I took a few boxes from the top shelf and heard the jingle of coins inside of purple and gold Crown Royal bag. I looked around to see if anyone heard me and thought I would steal it but no one was around. I picked the bag up and couldn't feel any coins. I felt bullets and a gun. I opened the bag and there it was the end of my misery. I wrapped the gun inside of a sweater and continued clean. When no one was looked I ran the sweater to my room and hid the gun under my bed.

Later that night I sat there, planning my suicide. I started to write....*By the time you read this I will be gone. I don't think you will miss me. I believe you have been trying to get me to reach my tragic end anyway so I wanted to make it easier for you. I hate you and I wish you were dead.*

I wanted to die when no one was around. I wanted them to find my body and I wanted them to see all they had done. I wanted the Coroner to inspect my body and see the wounds I had all over and make the obvious conclusion as to why I committed suicide.

I started to think if I ended my life Mama and Jerry would be happy. Plus, I've never shot a gun before. Now I'm afraid that I'll mess up and just injure myself for life. So, I started to research other ways of committing suicide that would be painless and swift. It was the only thing I could think about. Day after day it consumed me, I didn't care about grades or school. I planned to take my life by the end of the week.

Chapter 5: While She Was Sobbing…Coming Out of Isolation

While she was sobbing, her godmother, who was a Fairy, appeared before her. "Cinderella," said the Fairy, "I am your godmother, and for the sake of your dear mamma I have come to cheer you up, so dry your tears; you shall go to the grand ball to-night, but you must do what I was going to tell you. Go into the garden and bring me the biggest pumpkin you can find."

Cinderella brought the finest that was there. Her godmother scooped it out very quickly, and then struck it with her wand, upon which it was changed into a beautiful coach. Afterwards, the old lady peeped into the mousetrap, where she found six mice. She tapped him or her lightly with her wand, and each mouse became a fine white horse. The rattrap contained two large rats; one of these she turned into a coachman, and the other into a postilion. The old lady then told Cinderella to go into the garden and seek for half-a-dozen lizards. These she changed into six footmen, dressed in the finest attire.

"You are too smart for this type of work. You need to put in more effort." I didn't argue or offer an explanation. I just nodded. She continued to pass out graded work that apparently no one did quite well on. "I'm disappointed in a lot of you," she told the class. "I can tell that you didn't study. But, we're going to retest next week. I suggest you all go home and study this weekend." She was always gracious. But this time her merciful attempt to salvage my success in her class was unnecessary.

Mrs. Austin always had assigned seats based on your last name. My last name started with an A, so I had the pleasure of sitting right in front of her desk. I could feel her eyes curiously fixated on me as she sat down. "Shaunte' I need to see you after class." I nodded in agreement and waited for the class to be over, anxiously awaiting our meeting. I never had to stay after class with a teacher. But, I wasn't fearful at all. Mrs. Austin was the most beautiful woman I had ever met. She was an African American woman but she had sandy blonde hair that she kept in a neat bun with sideswiped bangs. She had beautiful greenish-gray eyes and always dressed modestly. She never raised her voice in class. She never had to. Her gentle and confident presence, commanded respect and order.

The bell rang and the students waited for her to dismiss. She ran a well-organized class. Even students that were horribly behaved in other classes knew to clean up their act with Mrs. Austin. "Have a great day, she said.

And in a rumble, the class grabbed their belongings and rushed into the tumultuous hallway filled with the laughter and chatter of hormone-raged teenagers.

"Lately, I've noticed a drop in your grades and efforts. What's going on?" she asked. I didn't have any response. My eyes welled up in tears. I was overcome with the grief of my coming end, the lost of my parents' love, the scars I was hiding on my skin and my heart. I dug my face into my hands as if I could hide there forever. She rubbed my back in consolation and I flinched at her touch. She jerked her hand away. Then, she cautiously brought it back soothingly and said, "Everything's going to be ok. You're going to make it. You're more than capable. A mind is a terrible thing to waste. And right now, that's what you're starting to do. Go to the restroom, clean your face and keep on moving forward."

"Give a man a fish and you feed him for a day; teach a man to fish and you feed him for a lifetime."

She changed everything for me just by caring. She took a few minutes out of her day to reach out to a student in need. That was her priority, meeting my need not my want. What I wanted was a new home, Mama to show me some form of affection, to not be the poor outcast. She did, however, give me what I needed: a way out. The idea that if I used my mind, the one thing that could never be taken from me, one day I would have my wants.

I went home and put that gun back in the closet. I didn't have better clothes but I started to piece what I did have together; to make it look a bit more attractive. I was tall for my age. Well, maybe not, but my pants said otherwise. I asked my sisters to come into my room to help me pick out clothes to get ready. Every pair of jeans was too short. We had the bright idea that if we cut two slits at the bottom of the pant legs, it would make them appear to be longer. We cut the bottom of a pair of white jeans and picked out a navy blue sweater with white and burgundy lines that ran horizontally across the chest. We paired it with a pair of platform Penny loafers that Mama got from Payless®. I tried the outfit on for my sisters. "What do you think," I asked. "You look cute," Maxine said. I smiled with glee.

The next day I walked confidently to the bus stop. Looking good and feeling good. We all caught the bus together: high school and intermediate school kids. Our school bus would drop off the intermediate school kids first at Coleman and then take us to "Chapel". While we were at the bus stop I could hear a few kids laughing at me. I ignored it; my self-esteem had taken a sure boost in a positive direction. I wouldn't let anyone ruin it. Once we were on the bus. My sisters and I sat in seats across from each other. Maxine and I taking the aisle seats while JJ and Joseline had window seats. Our shoes exposed in the aisle. A boy started making comments loud enough for me to hear, "Man, it's gon' rain today. I think it might *flood.*" Now I knew they were laughing at me.

My pants were too short and my clothes were outdated. We had never been to the mall to get clothes. All of our clothes came from rummage sales. Jerry would go out on Saturday mornings and get the family clothes. We had no say in what we wore. Not even Mama. Jerry was the only person allowed to buy clothes from department stores.

One girl made a comment that didn't live in our neighborhood. She didn't even live in our district. She would come to her grandmother's to catch the bus. Her grandmother owned a huge brick house at the end of the street. It had a built-in swimming pool and a basketball court. I didn't know her too well but my friend Veronica did. Surprisingly but not, Veronica didn't stand up for me. She laughed along with the others. *Keep moving forward*, I told myself. *Keep moving forward.*

"Aww man, look at the little one," she said pointing to our shoes. "She's just as bad as the big one. With those dirty FILA's on. Girl you need to throw those shoes in the trash." (The little one being my little sister Maxine.) People could talk about me all they wanted to. But there was no way I was going to let someone pick on my little sister. I told Joseline to come and sit with JJ so I could sit with Maxine.

I whispered to her, "Let's switch shoes."

"Why?"

"Because I need to have on tennis shoes."

"Please don't fight, you're going to get in trouble."

"I don't care, no one picks on you."

"Aww she switched shoes with the little one," the boy said. "So, she still looks a mess," the girl responded.

Mama had taken me out of band when my grades started to slip. Instead she put me in Study Hall for first period. The girl was also in band first period. My plan was to beat her with her on clarinet case when she got out of class. I sat in Study Hall the entire time charging up; letting all of my anger and frustration with life build into a roaring, American rage eagerly waiting to be unleashed.

When the bell rang to release first period I bee-lined to the breezeway that connected the location of the band room and the Jr. High School. Jarring through the crowds not caring who I bumped into, I looked for her. I started to get some attention. Teenagers can always sense when something was about to go down and I wanted an audience. Our eyes connected at the same time. She was no more than 5 yards in front of me. "You still talking *cuss*?!" I yelled. "What? Girl I'm not even paying you any attention," she said as she turned her back to me. Oh no, it's to late for that I want a fight and it's going to happen one way or another.

I ran into her punching her in the back of the head. She turned around. "Oh its on now," she said. The kids started yelling. "Fight! Fight! Fight! Fight!" I held my fists up, squaring up with her. Having no idea how to fight. I just figured I'd punch, scratch, pull her hair, go medieval and bite her if I had to.

I let out a belting scream and started swinging. We were tussling and tussling. I got a fist full of her hair and was out of breath. Fighting wore me out so fast. I figured I'd pull her hair with one hand, punch with the other and knee her in the face intermittently.

Then the tallest male teacher in the school came to break it up. He pulled her away from me, leaving my hands full of her hair. But giving her some leverage because then she kicked me in the face. I ran over to them both and started back fighting her while the teacher held her. I tugged at her shirt and bra until I pulled them both off. Well they didn't come completely off. The bra did, but the shirt was pulled over her back and unto her arms. Which were left dangling over her head while she ran around blinded by the front of her shirt. The teacher didn't dare touch a bare-chested girl.

I shamed her. That's what she did to my little sister and me. She shamed us, so I felt obliged to return the favor.

When we got to the Principal's office I felt relieved and embarrassed. Mrs. Austin had just told me about "moving forward and working hard". The Principal was surprised to see both of us. I had never been in any trouble at school. The girl hadn't either. "Why were you two fighting?" he asked. She was picking on my little sister on the school bus," I answered. "Is this true?" he asked the girl. "Yes," she responded, "but the other kids were too." "Well I'm going to suspend both of you for three days. Fighting is not the answer and following the wrong crowd isn't either."

We waited for our parents to pick us up and to receive our work that we would be missing over the next few days. I opened my English book and there was a note from Mrs. Austin. *I'm very disappointed in you.* Then, Mama came and picked me up. We walked to the car in silence. Once I got in the back seat my sisters were there. "They told me what happened," Mama said. Apparently my sisters called Mama when they got to school, upset at what had happened on the bus. Mama picked them up from school and then got the call about my fight.

"Well you're gonna be at home for three days. Do all of your work and stay out of trouble. I don't want to keep missing out on work because of this." *Phew, saved by the sisters.*

Once we were home for about an hour there was a knock on the door. It was the girl and her mother. "Hi, I'm Brenda. I'm Naomi's mother. They got into a fight today." "Yeah I know," Mama said. "Well they don't need to be fighting. One day they're fighting and the next day, they're best friends. And I'm gonna make sure they are friends. Ya'll come on and shake hands and make up," Brenda said.

What!? She wants me to be this girl's friend. I don't want her touching me and I don't want to touch her. From the look on her face, she felt the same. But we shook hands in a truce.

Ms. Brenda meant every word of what she said. Naomi and I were forced friends. Brenda would come and pick me up on the weekends. I would come to their house for sleepovers and family outings.

One day she took us to Boo at the Zoo in Little Rock, Arkansas. Not to have fun, but to work. "You have to learn how to make your own money," she said. She would get us all kinds of little jobs on the weekend: cleaning, babysitting and even working at carnivals. It was the most time I had spent out of the house and away from my family. It really opened my eyes to a different world. Brenda was affectionate and strong. Her kids had nice things but they also worked for it. I learned responsibility from her. I developed my sense of responsibility and independence.

On Saturdays when I was with Naomi she went to her grandmother's house. Her grandmother was Dr. Green. She was the superintendent at one of the local school districts. The inside of her house was even more spectacular than I had imagined.

Dr. Green was very kind and accepting to me. She was also brilliant. She had several framed degrees on the walls and beautiful family pictures. Her house was so clean and smelled so good. I never wanted to leave. She set up a guest room for me beside Naomi's.

The next morning was Sunday and we were going to her church. I didn't have any church clothes, so Naomi let me borrow one of her dresses. I had never been to church in Pine Bluff before. I was nervous as to what to do and what to say. I figured I would just smile and keep quiet.

When we woke up we had breakfast at the family table, also a new thing for me. At home we always grabbed our plates and went into our rooms to eat. We took showers, got dressed and got into her grandmother's showroom

SUV and headed to Old St. James Missionary Baptist Church.

Everyone was very nice and greeted me as I entered the church. I sat with Naomi at the back. This was where all of the teenage members sat and apparently lot of other kids from my school. Dr. Green was an Usher so she stood at the door.

When service began, someone directed us to stand and receive the choir. We stood and Dr. Green opened the back doors. The choir was dressed in beautiful gold and burgundy robes with the letters OSJ stitched on their lapels. The leader raised her right hand and they began to march down the aisles singing, "Praise Jehovah, He's the Great I AM". The choir sang angelically and for the first time, in a long time I felt safe. Safe and free.

Chapter 6: Glass Slippers…Combat Boots

When all these things had been done, the kind godmother touching her with her wand changed her worn-out clothes into a beautiful ball-dress embroidered with pearls and silver. She then gave her a pair of glass slippers, that is, they were woven of the most delicate spun glass, fine as the web of a spider.

At the end of my eighth grade year I was taking a class called Career Planning taught by Mrs. Berry. She would expose us to various careers and their paths to success. She also taught us the process of taking and earning enough credits to graduate. After all, next year we would start our official journey to high school graduation. In her class we would have the chance to build our own schedule and select electives. Some kids would choose a sport, band or an art class as their elective.

Another option, that was only available to you when you started the ninth grade, was Army JROTC. Two students along with their Senior Army Instructor came to our class one day to talk about JROTC. My eyes lit up like Christmas trees when I saw those kids walk in with all of those medals on their chest. Colonel Antee, Zedralyn Butler, and Brandy Sanders walked into my eighth grade classroom and changed my paradigm. I wanted to be like those girls. Zedralyn mesmerized me. She was smart and she played basketball, why did she need JROTC?

I needed to step my game up. Band was taking from me and I couldn't afford to be in any sports. With JROTC, I would get a free uniform, earn credits toward graduation and gain a sense of self-pride. I filled out my schedule in haste. Took it home to get Mama's approval, which luckily, she accepted. My grades had improved. I was back to being a straight A student, this wouldn't cost any money so there was no reason to deny my request. But she did warn when she signed my permission slip, "If your grades start to slip, I'm pulling you out of this too." "It won't Mama, this is a class. I'll be sure to keep my grades straight A's"

This is where I started to receive recognition for my hard work: my ninth grade year of high school. I became very competitive. Straight A's even in my AP classes. I worked hard in class and gained the favor of my teachers. Each and every day I was anxious to get to fifth period, JROTC, Echo Company. I lived for JROTC. The harder I worked the more ribbons I received. By the end of the year my chest was full of ribbons and at the end of the year banquet I received the highest honor: the Superior Cadet Award. Mama came to the banquet with me. She smiled and gave me a standing ovation when they called my name. My sisters and JJ were there too. I had fallen back into the good graces of Mama. I was on a steamroller to a bright future and I wasn't about to slow down.

When I turned 16 I asked Mama and Jerry if I could get a job. "Sure," they answered, "as long as your grades don't slip." At this point I had a 4.3 GPA, I was in high school and it was time I started making my own money. I wanted to buy my own school clothes and better feminine products. Jerry would buy one big pack of sanitary napkins a month from Fred's General Store for all of the ladies in the house to share. One day I went to the nurse's office for some and she gave me a brand name product that changed my life. I just had to get a job and have my own money to get the things I wanted and needed.

Finally, I landed my first job, working at the local Taco Bell. Jerry or Mama agreed to pick me up at work. They still didn't trust me to get a ride with someone else and after four long weeks of hard work, I had earned my first paycheck. Jerry took me to pick up my first check after school on a Friday. I came back to the car so elated and before I could open it up to see how much it was Jerry had demanded, "Now you gotta give me $64 every time you get paid. You have to start paying rent and helping out around the house." *Rent?! Is he serious?* So I opened up my check to discover that those hours added up to $121.64 after taxes and I had to give Jerry $64. That left me with $57.64. Barely enough money to do anything with.

Every two weeks Jerry would take me to pick up my check and take it to get cashed at the bank. He never came to any of my award ceremonies or school functions but he was always willing to take money from me when I got paid. I despised him for that. I wanted to ask Mama for a reduction in this so called "rent". Especially since it came with no extra privileges.

I went into her room to talk and I saw her rolling pennies into fifty-cent coin rollers. "Hey Mama, what are you up to?" "I'm rolling some pennies so I can go up to Sav-U-More to get some bread." "I gave Daddy $64 today." "Oh. Well I ran out of my $20, I'll ask him for more money when he gets home."

Mama had opened up to me about money, which was usually not discussed with the children, and it infuriated me. Jerry did not work, at all. Mama worked a state job making $32,000 a year. But was given $20 every two weeks to live off of. When she ran out of her "allowance" she had to use Jerry's pocket change that he would dump on the dresser when he got home at night.

"Here Mama." I gave her $10. "Just use this for bread." "Oh thanks baby. I'll give you your change." "Don't worry about it Mama."

Jerry was taking my money and hers and there was nothing we could do about it. She couldn't help me. She couldn't even help herself. I guess because Jerry was the "Man of the House" he got to decide where the money went. But, I still felt it was unfair. We still didn't have many groceries at home. Our diet consisted of rice, hot dogs and chicken. Sometimes if we were lucky we got sausage and cereal. My best meals came out of that Watson Chapel High School cafeteria. The bonus was my new job working at Taco Bell. I got a discount on food and would bring it home to family whenever I got a chance.

When I was a junior in high school I started to talk to an Army recruiter. He had told me about a program the Army had called the Delayed Entry Program for the Army Reserves. I could join the Army during my junior year and go to Basic Training the summer before my senior year started. I told Mama I was thinking about it. "Well that's up to you. But, that's a serious choice to make. Think about it long and hard before you choose," Mama said.

September 11, 2001 at 9:00 a.m. I was walking to Mrs. Word's AP History class when the fire alarms went off. We were all told to get into our designated tornado drill safety posts. The TV's in our school were set up on some sort of crossbar switch. In an instant all TV's were on and the scene before my eyes made my heart drop into my stomach. We're being bombed I thought. You could hear teachers and students crying in disbelief. We were being attacked. America was under attack. There is an arsenal in my city so people were terrified and on high alert. My choice was clear now. I'm joining the Army.

15 November 2001, four days after my 17th birthday, I raised my right hand and said, "I, Shaunte' Donisha-Lete' Anderson, do solemnly swear that I will support and defend the Constitution of the United States against all enemies, foreign and domestic; that I will bear true faith and allegiance to the same; and that I will obey the orders of the President of the United States and the orders of the officers appointed over me, according to regulations and the Uniform Code of Military Justice. So help me God."

Joining the Army was a bold move on my part in the eyes of my JROTC instructors. That year I served as the Cadet Command Sergeant Major. Usually the cadet/CSM advanced to the position of Battalion Commander their senior year. But, there were other students hoping to knock me out of position.

My leadership skills were in question. I didn't know how to delegate responsibilities effectively. I also had a huge alpha female persona, which made a lot of cadets not want to work with me. I started to become an unapproachable leader.

After the suggestion of my Army Instructor Sergeant Major Edwards, I humbled myself and realized that I was a student like they were. I could lose my position as easy as it was handed to me. But, my changes had seemed to come too late.

There was a rumor that two of my classmates were up for Battalion Commander, that even though I was the Command Sergeant Major, I would be promoted to the Battalion Executive Officer. A step below the Battalion Commander. Colonel Warrick and Sergeant Major Edwards had a meeting with me the day before our end of the year Promotion and Awards Ceremony.

"We wanted to talk to you before the ceremony. Lately, you've become hard to work with. We need a leader that we can trust, someone that can carry out his or her duties effectively and with honor. There are two other cadets that we are considering for Battalion Commander next year. We think it would be best if you were the Battalion XO next year. Are you ok with that?"

My heart was racing at the beginning of our meeting and then it felt like every major organ in my body had shut down. Time had stood still while they were waiting for my answer. My initial answer was: "No, I didn't work harder than every cadet, sacrifice more than every cadet or give my all to this program to not obtain the highest level possible. It was my plan from the beginning to have my picture on the wall and made an eternal part of the battalion".

But then I thought about all I had gained during the program, a higher sense of self. After all I had just joined the Army in November and one of the Army's Core Values is Selfless Service. That meant to…"Put the welfare of the nation, the Army and your subordinates before your own. Selfless service is larger than just one person. In serving your country, you are doing your duty loyally without thought of recognition or gain. The basic building block of selfless service is the commitment of each team member to go a little further, endure a little longer, and look a little closer to see how he or she can add to the effort." ("ARMY.MIL Features")
So my final answer was, "Yes, I'll be here and I will support whomever you select."

The next night we were at the Promotions and Awards Ceremony. I walked with dignity and pride in my uniform; my chest was full of medals and honorable badges, each shoulder draped with a distinct cord. Last year, I got the Superior Cadet award for the second time. Everyone in the room knew that was an indicator that I would be promoted to the Command Sergeant Major. I would be the leader in charge of all the Battalion's special teams. I was also apart of the Battalion Headquarters.

This year the time had arrived to award the highest honors: the Superior Cadet award. They announced the winner...a fellow classmate of mine. His faced flushed red with gratification as he came to attention and marched forward to receive his award. He never came back to his seat, but stood to the side of the awards table because the very next phase of the ceremony was to announce the new battalion commander and his staff.

Lieutenant Colonel Warrick grabbed the list of promotions and with a stern voice said, "The 2002-2003 Watson Chapel Sr. High School Battalion Commander is: Shaunte' Anderson." It took my breath away. It was a test. That entire meeting was a test of my commitment to the program. And I passed. They invited Mama to come and change my ranks from Command Sergeant Major to Lieutenant Colonel. I started to hold back my tears and show no emotion. But I didn't. I let the tears run warm, single streams down each cheek. I loved this program and I worked hard to obtain this goal. I was ready to serve it with all that I had. There was no better choice than me and I was going to work to hard to solidify my selection.

Welcome to Fort Leonard Wood, the sign read. I had attended a mock boot camp a few years ago at Fort Leonard Wood so I was clear of my expectations. I was assigned to Bravo 1/148 under the direction of Drill Sergeant Love and Drill Sergeant Wood (no pun intended).

The first days of boot camp I wondered, *what did I get myself into?* As the days turned into weeks my body and my mind grew stronger. During the last month of basic training I started to have horrible pain in my legs each morning. I had been to sick call a few times before with leg complaints. The treatment was clear: take ibuprofen and ice my legs at night. But each morning I still found it hard to walk. My battle buddy switched bunks with me so that I was now sleeping on the bottom bunk to mask my difficulty with getting out of bed each day.

One week before graduation we were going on our final battalion run. My injury had become more obvious to my Drill Sergeants who decided to put me in front so that I would not be left behind. My run time had slowed when it should have increased. I could barely walk. I had no clue how I was going to run. But here goes nothing.

"Left, face." "Forward, march," Drill Sergeant Love commanded. We left the barracks and headed to the running trail. "Column, Left," drill sergeant ordered. The soldier behind me unaware of my slower tempo, stepped on the back of my shoes. My heel lifted out of them and powerlessly I fell, my shins breaking my fall against the cement curbside. My legs started to bleed from the fall. "What a waste," Drill Sergeant Love said.

I was transported to the hospital to get x-rays. "You have stress fractures," the doctor said. Both my tibia and fibula bones in each leg were fractured. That explained why I could barely use them but I was so upset at the fact that it was a week before graduation and I was missing it.

I came back home a few days after school had started, still on two crutches, unable to walk. The questions and jokes were never ending but I kept striving I did more with my summer than most kids have done their whole lives. The Army gave me a Line of Duty form to be seen once I got home and allowed me to come back next summer to finish basic where I left off.

When I came home I took my senior pictures and shopped at the mall for the first time. I didn't give Jerry a dime of my earnings. After basic training, I was determined to not be taken advantage of again. I literally milked that whole situation. No one in my family had ever been to the Army before so they had no clue of what it entailed. I came back and acted like I was a stone-cold killer. Whenever, I rode in the car with Mama or Jerry I would whip out my black-blade folding knife. Mama asked me one day, "why do you have that knife out?" "I need it. If we get in an accident I need to be able to cut myself out of the seat belt," I snarled.

I loved that knife. Frankly, if Jerry had of attempted to hit me again I would have stabbed him with it. I had become quite fearless after training. Since then the Army has discontinued the Delayed Entry Program for reasons unknown to me. But, one thing is for sure I felt out of place going from Army life to high school life overnight.

By the end of my senior year I had a 4.1 GPA, a 24 on the ACT and acceptance letters from the schools I wanted to attend. I figured I would use my GI Bill to pay for school but that meant starting school a semester later than I had planned.

One day I got a letter in the mail from the University of Arkansas at Pine Bluff. They had awarded me the University Scholarship and the Academic scholarship: a "full ride" to college. It was completely taboo to go to UAPB at my school. My entire high school career the counselors and teachers would warn the black students. "UAPB is a party school. Don't go there. Go to Arkansas State or if you're really special the University of Arkansas at Fayetteville." But, those schools didn't offer me any scholarships or showed interest in the student-leader that I was. I decided to go to the school that seemed to value me before I had even stepped a foot on their campus: I'm going to "The Yard".

Chapter 7: The Ball…Welcome to The Yard

On her arrival, her beauty struck everybody with wonder. The gallant Prince gave her a courteous welcome, and led her into the ball-room; and the King and Queen were as much enchanted with her, as the Prince conducted her to the supper-table, and was too much occupied in waiting upon her to partake of anything himself. While seated, Cinderella heard the clock strike three-quarters past eleven.

The day had finally arrived: UAPB Freshmen Move-in Day. I woke up at 6:00 AM. All of my belongings were already packed and waiting in my 1992 Nissan Sentra. The only thing I had to do was shower, get dressed and step into my new beginning. I had spent the entire summer intermittently watching the UAPB channel on cable all summer. Channel 24 had become my new favorite. They showcased their choir, football team, STEM program; all of the great programs they had to offer.

An hour had passed and everyone was sleep but my sisters. I was waiting for my parents to wake. I was sure that they would assist me in moving into my dorm room. I was the first person in the family to go to college. This was a big day for me, for all of us.

I went to Mama's door and knocked. "Hey Mama I'm ready." I didn't expect Jerry to come. He hadn't come to any of my functions. Ever. But, I had a glimmer of hope that he would at least come this time. "Call me when you get there," Mama said. I didn't allow their rejection to sadden me. I had no room for disappointment today. I hopped in my car and rode off into the sunset.

To my surprise there were fraternities and sororities there helping the freshmen move in to their rooms. I was assigned to the Harrold Complex in the Johnson and Copeland Halls. It was the closest thing to having my own place. I went to the front desk picked up my keys and went to my room. I loved it! I was full of excitement and joy.

There were many other girls moving in as well. Everyone was so different. The mass majority of girls were African-American but in a variation of ways I had never seen. Southern girls, northern girls, girls from Jamaica, girls from Africa, privileged girls and girls from humble beginnings.

I skipped down the stairs with glee to get more boxes. As I walked back to my dorm to my pleasant surprise members of one of the fraternities offered me help. "Where are your parents?" One of the guys asked. "Oh, I'm from here so I didn't need any help." He just shrugged and helped me get my things to my room.

Common sense told me, "*Look these guys prey on naïve freshmen like you. So don't think you're someone special. Just accept the help and move on.*" But my hormones said, *"Who cares! He's fine and if he asks you out say yes! Well, play hard to get but not to hard.* I figured my hormones were right and dated this guy for about two months. And so it began. I let my hormones control much of my college matriculation.

Still, I wanted to be involved as much as possible. My college experience was going to be what I made and I wanted an experience of a lifetime. Freshmen year, I had the grand idea to run for class president. I didn't win but I became a Student Senator and ultimately the Student Senate Pro Temp. At the time the University had risen in its NCAA Division and had began to add new sports to include Women's Golf and Women's Soccer. I was never an athlete but had dreams of being a part of a team. One day fter class I changed into work out clothes and found out where the soccer team was holding practice. I asked the Coach if he still need members and he answered in a Nigerian accent,

"Have you ever played soccer?"

"No."

"Can you run?"

"Yes."

"Practice with us today and I'll see."

I ran the hardest I had in my life and I got a couple of lucky kicks. I wasn't the best he had seen but this was a new program and he needed the players. Not long after, I was in his office picking up my uniform. We had gotten new uniforms sponsored by Puma®. I held up the Black and Gold jersey with the number 20 on the back with a great sense of thankfulness.

Finally, someone gave me a chance. One Nigerian coach in Pine Bluff, Arkansas gave me a chance and opened the door to endless opportunities. Later, I would become the first African-American Girls' Soccer Head Coach in the Suburban North of St. Louis, Missouri and play for the Women's Island Soccer Association in Hawaii.

I was all about obtaining things that people said I couldn't do and being a college athlete was just the start. Ladies of virtue, strength and influence were often times members of the first sorority for African-American women. Many of the women I looked up to in my personal life were also members of the same sorority. It was my dream to be found amongst the greats. During the spring semester of my sophomore year, I expressed my interest and was accepted into that Sorority. It was truly one of the highlights of my college career.

A distinct honor and privilege it was to rub shoulders with the beautiful and talented women of such a grand organization. I loved my line sisters and treasured them so much. I had their back and they had mine. I had never had such acceptance and loyalty.

Feeling as though I had "arrived", I earned the title of Super Greek by a rival sorority. I took it as a compliment. In my eyes I had finally attained the unattainable: status.

Athlete. Scholar. Sorority Girl. Student Senator. Tutor. Legion of Valor recipient. I wore these framed accomplishments on the outside. But on the inside was a dirty, insecure girl curled in fetal position waiting to be rescued. And if you looked closer you would see the words: whore, filthy, unloved, neglected, unwanted, fake, pathetic, stupid, needy, and desperate branded into her flesh so that it is never forgotten or erased.

Chapter 8: The Clock Struck Twelve…Darkness Returns

To her alarm she heard the clock strike twelve. She fled from the ball-room; but in a moment the coach changed again to a pumpkin, the horses to mice, the coachman and postilion to rats, the footmen to lizards, and Cinderella's beautiful dress to her old shabby clothes. In her haste she dropped one of her glass slippers, and reached home, out of breath, with none of her godmother's fairy gifts but one glass slipper.

I did it. I crossed the great moat that had for centuries succeeded at defeating my family's will to overcome. With all its splendor, the mote, by shear intimidation, pierced the hearts and minds of those before me. It dealt a blow so powerful, many had refused to allow any thought of crossing it a possibility. It should have perpetuated a delay in my advancement, but it failed. I stood chest up, shoulders back and eyes to the sky. I held in my hand the key to success, the key that would unlock the door of the prison called predestined poverty and lock the door behind me as I strutted through with confidence: my college degree.

Be it as it may at my college graduation, I wept. I had no clue why I had such an emotional attachment to my fellow classmates, because I never cried at my high school graduation. The anticipation of finally leaving my parents and getting out on my own, wouldn't allow me. But here, in this moment, the thoughts and energy are so overwhelming. What am I going to do when I leave here? What does life after college look like?

I had done all the right things at the wrong time. I had not followed the pertinent advice of those selected to steward my college matriculation. Instead, I did just enough to get by academically and more than enough to get by socially.

The last year of my college education was a blur. I felt like I had went through some sort of Dorothy, Wizard of Oz tornado and it dropped me into a stadium during college graduation. And I'm clicking my BCBG's in hopes of returning to Emerald City. Instead, I'm here, back where I started, with a suitcase and three garbage bags of clothes and shoes. I'm sitting in the back seat of "the Lesabre". Lord give me strength. Here I am squished in the back seat with my two little sisters and my step-brother. We were four full-sized children sitting behind our parents. This is not what I expected after graduation.

Most people are with their families, out to dinner at one of the two restaurants in the city. But, not me I'm just beginning the first event of my inevitable post-graduation depression.

We pull up to our home and for the first time I realize that I have an insurmountable hate in my heart for the powder pink trim that beams so joyfully to passersby. It was just as out of place as I. Who would put powder pink trim on a house with black shingles and tombstone gray stairs?

I thought I would never have to live another day in this house. Why, oh why did I waste my opportunity? I had it made for four years. I had a nice place to live, fancy car, became a member of the best sorority, played college soccer and even had a couple of good-looking boyfriends.

"And I gave my heart to seek and search out by wisdom concerning all things that are done under heaven: this sore travail hath God given to the sons of man to be exercised therewith. I have seen all the works that are done under the sun; and, behold, all is vanity and vexation of spirit." Ecclesiastes 1:13-14

No party tonight for me. I wanted to slip out of the memory of my classmates as soon as possible. Give myself enough time to reconvene at the drawing board of my life. I needed a new plan and I needed it fast. The after-thought of my college career was dramatically strangling

"I should have spent my Junior and Senior years going on internships and interviews."

"I should have joined that LSAT study group. Instead I partied and the worst part I worked a job."

"I worked so much during college."

I would have let this never ending mental Ping-Pong go on forever. But I called a time-out to sit and chat with my first and only best friends—my sisters. I had been so consumed with my plans and myself. I was truly curious as to what life had been like for them while I was "away" at college.

I have always been over protective of my little sisters. I was their unofficial and understood bodyguard. Although they had had the favoritism of my parents, I would soon learn that they were not granted asylum from my stepfather's dictatorship.

The one place of somewhat safety and liberty in my parents' home was our bedrooms. This is subsequently, the place where conspiracy theories were confirmed as realities. I looked to my sisters and finally broke the silence. "So what's been going on lately?"

Before anyone could answer, Joseline went into the living room to make sure the coast was clear to talk. "Well," Maxine started, "Daddy texted this guy that I'm dating about watching gay pornography." "What!" I exclaimed. "He's sick. Why would he ask him that? Did he say?" "No," Maxine answered. "And, there's a gay guy at my school. We're in band together. He said that he's friends with Daddy on Facebook and he messaged him the same question."

The rumors and speculations had started to make sense. People in town even some of my cousins had said there was a rumor that Jerry was on the down low. How embarrassing? My anger burned red hot. My plan was to start an argument and get him to confess out of emotion.

When Jerry got home. I went to the kitchen to get a glass of water. He was sitting on the couch watching TV. "Mama, did you hear about Maxine's boyfriend," I yelled across the house. "What!" she responded. "Can you come in here," I requested. "Yeah I heard he's been getting strange messages about pornography. He said he got it from Daddy," I said. "You don't have to speak over me," Jerry replied.

"Oh, so it's true?"

"Is what true?"

"You're sending homosexuals messages about porno."

"I don't think that's any of your business."

"Wow. Ok. That's how they do it."

"Well, I was just trying to see where his head was at."

"And what was that supposed to prove?"

Jerry was so mad but I didn't care. He had gone to far and I was gonna go with him. Everyone just started arguing. Mama, my sisters, me, everyone. I looked at the table that had a Bible on it. Jerry had become an ordained minister a few years ago, which made no sense to me. He only had a 6th grade education and never went to church. While I was "away" at college he was trying to build a church and preach. I never went to hear any of his sermons. As far as I could tell he had made no changes. He was still addicted to porn, gambling, mistreating his wife and now involved with young men. He wasn't fooling me. He could fool anybody else who was gullible enough to believe he was a man of God, but not me. Not any of my siblings.

I picked up the Bible and said, "What we need to do is open this Bible and have some real preaching in here!" I knew I had struck a nerve. Jerry charged at me, "What you trying to say. I ain't real?"

"Please stop spitting on me. When you talk, you spit."

"Well I guess you just know it all then. Since you went to "college". What you can do is get out of my house."

"Gladly," I said.

"No, no," Maxine said. "You always push her away. Please don't go." Everyone just paused at those words. Mama took control of the situation, "Everybody just need to calm down and go to their rooms. These are nothing but ugly rumors."

I went to the room infuriated. I got him to confess but it didn't accomplish or resolve anything.

Chapter 9: One Day Prince Charming Will Come…The Prophecy

When her sisters arrived after the ball, they spoke in terms of rapture of the unknown Princess, and told Cinderella about the little glass slipper she had dropped, and how the Prince picked it up. It was evident to all the Court that the Prince was determined if possible, to find out the owner of the slipper; and a few days afterwards a royal herald proclaimed that the King's son would marry her whose foot the glass slipper should be found exactly to fit. Prince Charming and his Grand Duke traveled from house to house looking for the owner of the glass slipper. But to no avail. One day Prince Charming arrived to the home Cinderella and her wicked stepfamily.

The next morning I flipped open my pink, Motorola Razor phone and searched for someone, anyone to talk to. Then I came to the name, Danielle. She was a co-worker of mine. She was a cool down-to-earth chick. I decided to give her a call. I knew she would listen without judgment.

"Everything is just so crazy right now," I said.

"Well I'm going to this church thing tonight. You wanna go?"

"Yes, girl. That's what I need: church."

I wore an all black knee-length dress. My eyelids were swollen from all the crying. My hair was pulled back in a messy bun, just like me a mess. We walked into this small church with about 25 people present. The music was playing softly but people were standing and worshipping while the guest preacher walked through the aisles and prayed for people.

Then, the preacher came to a woman a few aisles ahead of me. "Lift your hands," he said. "You're having troubles with your womanly organs. You can't have a baby. But it's because of something you did. You caused it. But, God said He's going to heal and you shall bring forth a child." The woman started crying and thanking God. Her husband held her as she bent over weeping in relief.

This man knew her entire life. He's a prophet! I had never met a prophet. I heard of them but honestly I didn't know they really existed. He prophesied to more people that wailed and praised God after he spoke to them. "Lift your hands everybody," he said. "God is not done yet." I lifted my hands slightly and squinted my eyes so that I could see what was going on. I was hoping and praying he would come to me. Give me some answers to what's going on in my life.

The prophet started to walk down my aisle. I stood their frozen with my hands up like I was about to be arrested. He grabbed my wrist and led me to the altar. Out of sheer emotion I began to cry, not knowing what was about to happen next. And then he began to speak: "You're at a crossroads right now and you don't know which way to go." He paused as if he was listening to someone standing over him. "There are two people in your life that are troubling you. God said you are like the Cinderella story, the Cinderella story gone wrong. But God told me to tell you that Cinderella's still going to the ball."

I hunched over and put my face into my hands and cried bitterly. I didn't question the process. I was just happy that somebody cared, not just anybody: God Almighty. He saw everything the good and the bad. All of my sins and flaws, yet he was still going to help me.

"Lift your head and raise your hands," he said. "I don't want to be a hypocrite," I responded. I knew that I was unworthy and sinful. He said, "This is just you surrendering to God." It made sense now. I never knew why people did that. I always thought they were trying to appear holier than others.

Yes, this is right. I need to surrender to God. No matter what I was trying to do, it didn't survive. I can't do it alone. I need Him. He's my only hope. He can do everything. He can do all things. Nothing shall be impossible to them that believe!

I raised my hands and fainted faster than I could catch myself. One the ushers came and laid a sheet over my legs. I laid there with my face stuck to that burgundy carpet and cried. I felt God holding me in consolation.

And then I heard the song. I couldn't understand the words at first and now it resonated so clear. The beat of the drums seemed to rattle my spirit. The song had come to a high point. All I could hear were the drums being struck with pure intensity and then with a sudden rest beat I could hear the choir: *Praise is what I dooooo! It's what I do.*

The drums kicked up again and the soloist declared: *I might be sick in my body so...Praise is what I do!...You may need healing in your mind, you might need healing in your spirit...Praise is what I do!* I just laid there still and a sweet lady kneeled down to me and said, "you just take your time baby." I just started bawling all over again. My moment was not being rushed. My touch from God was not being rushed. It was everything I ever needed.

Chapter 10: Happily Ever After…By the Blood of the Lamb and the Word of Her Testimony

This proclamation caused a great sensation. Ladies of all ranks were permitted to make a trial of the slipper; but it was of no use. Cinderella now said, "Let me try—perhaps it may fit me." It slipped on in a moment. Great was the vexation of the two sisters at this; but what was their astonishment when Cinderella took the fellow slipper out of her pocket! At that moment the godmother appeared, and touched Cinderella's clothes with her wand. Her sisters then saw that she was the beautiful lady they had met at the ball, and, throwing themselves at her feet, craved her forgiveness.

The next week I was accepted into Graduate School at Webster University in St. Louis, Missouri. Since I had not gotten into the Law School of my choice I decided to work on a Master's in Legal Analysis. These were all moves in a positive direction for me. All was not lost after all. God was true to his Word.

The most remarkable aspects of living in the campus apartments were my roommates. Each of my roommates was from a different county: Japan, China and Thailand. I had read a poster once that said, "A smile is the same in every language." I needed that tidbit of advice often. We tried each other's food. Sometimes we liked it, sometimes we didn't. The one thing that was constant was a respect for each other's culture. I loved the experience and the exposure. It was a stark contrast from my time at an HBCU. But I had a great foundation of my own culture first which helped me to appreciate others.

A few months into my program I was hired as a Student Services Coordinator at the University of Phoenix. And when I wasn't there I interned for a Lawyer downtown. Things were starting to pull together nicely.

At the University of Phoenix I assisted the teachers and worked at the front desk answering phones and greeting prospective and current students. One day a lady walked in the door with the most beautiful hair. She had an interview with one of the College Coordinators to talk about enrolling into a program. The person she had the interview with was late so we sat and talked about everything and nothing.

What I really wanted to know was, who did her hair? I was still new to the area and was in need of a trustworthy beautician. "My daughter does my hair," she said.

"She's in cosmetology school. Do you have a church home yet?" She spared no time getting that question in but I was glad she asked. I had visited a few places but none seemed to be a fit. "You should come to visit my church one day. Call me and I'll give you directions."

Two weeks later I decided to visit that church. But it didn't look like the church I was expecting. It was located in a small trip mall between a used car lot and a Mexican grocery store. When I walked in the door I didn't see the typical church. They had lined four rows of off white office chairs for seating. The pastor stood on a makeshift platform with two statement chairs behind him and spoke from a small hand carved podium. There were about twenty members present

It definitely wasn't what I expected and although it didn't look like a church, it felt like a church. The sweetest feeling of peace came over me when I walked into that building, but I was still very skeptical. I would only come to the Bible Study on Wednesday nights and even then I would be an hour late. In the short time I was present I had learned so much in a class taught by the first lady called "A Search for Truth II".

Being in the Legal Studies program, I developed an ultra investigative and research approach to new material. I refused to believe and accept anything the first lady taught before investigating it myself. The Bible Study was taught on a large flip chart supported on an easel. I would right down every scripture on the chart and then spend the next week reading and researching to see if it was true. The next Wednesday I would come back hungry for more.

"Search the scriptures; for in them ye think ye have eternal life: and they are they which ***testify of me****."*
John 5:39

After about two months I was encouraged to come to a Sunday service. The worship service was like nothing I had ever experienced. The Pastor's wife was the only one who sang on the platform but the entire congregation sang along with her. People started shouting, jumping and speaking in tongues. That's when I noticed it; none of the women in this church wore pants and when they started speaking in tongues I thought, *this is one of those sanctified churches*. I had never been to a sanctified church before and I actually enjoyed it.

My life truly began to change. I would stay up late at night to read the scriptures I wrote from the previous Bible study. Studying alone, started to create a gap between the life I used to live and the one that had suddenly overtaken me.

One Wednesday night after Bible Study was over. I stayed behind in the classroom to do some reading over what was taught. Jesus spoke to me, "Shaunte', I'm God." The Pastor's wife walked in a second later and I just yelled, "JESUS is GOD!!" "Yes, Shaunte' Jesus is God!" "I need to get baptized," I said, "I want His name on me. I need to be baptized in Jesus' name!"

"When they heard this, they were baptized in the name of the Lord Jesus."
Acts 19:5

"Next you'll be ready for the Holy Ghost," the Pastor's wife said. "I already have the Holy Ghost," I told her matter of factly. "You do?" she asked. "Yep" "Well how do you know?" "Well one day I fainted and cried. That's the Holy Ghost right?" "Just keep reading," she said.

"He said unto them, Have ye received the Holy Ghost since ye believed? And they said unto him, We have not so much as heard whether there be any Holy Ghost."
Acts 19:2

On Friday, I went to an Anthony Hamilton concert at an annual event in St. Louis called the LouFest. Anthony invited his wife to come up and sing. She's a gospel singer and the entire audience started worshipping and singing along with her. I told God, "Lord it would be great if I could worship with a group of black people on Sunday." Our church was small and I found comfort in there being more people around.

That Sunday, July 3, 2008, we had visitors. A group of young black people from a church in Clarksville, Tennessee. *God has a sense of humor*. But, what struck me was the worship of this one girl named Shekinah. We were about the same age naturally but spiritually she was years ahead of me. When worship started she sang like there was no one in the room but her and God. She paced in front of the platform singing and waving her hands in the air. During the last song she laid on the ground and cried out to God. I looked at her and said God I want that. I want to worship like there's no one around but You and me.

After service I was to be baptized in Jesus' name at a local church, since our church didn't have a baptismal. I invited Shekinah and her friends to ride with me to the church. She shared with me her experiences and how she received the Holy Ghost at a young age in the church bathroom. I wanted that so bad. A relationship with God. She told me to just reach out to God and worship with all my might when I was raised from the water of my baptism to receive the Holy Ghost.

We got to the church, prayed and they sent me off to change. I was so nervous, but ready. I had repented of my sins and committed myself to living for God. As I stepped into the water it was comforting and warm. I thought it would be cold. But the water eased my anxiety. I can't swim so being immersed in water terrifies me. The Pastor assured me that he would catch me. Everyone started praying for me and then the Pastor began to pray and make an announcement in the lines of: according to the confession of your faith, I now baptize you in the name of Jesus for the remission of your sins and you shall receive the gift of the Holy Ghost. I went down in the water, symbolizing the death of the old me and then I was raised out of the water symbolizing the resurrection of the new me in Christ. I now bore the name of Jesus Christ.

I came out of that water hollering like a mad woman. But no Holy Ghost. I had realized now what receiving the Holy Ghost would be but I was afraid. I thought it would hurt or burn. I thought I would lose control of myself in a seizure. I was just analyzing everything. I wanted to know how it would happen and what it would be like. I seemed I could where clothes like a Pentecostal, study the Bible and worship but I wouldn't get the Holy Ghost. I thought: *I'm not good enough yet.*

The next Sunday we had a guest speaker. He spoke a powerful message and at the end he spoke about his experience with receiving the Holy Ghost. How it took him so long to receive It. He talked about his personality and thoughts. How he overanalyzed the entire situation, but finally he gave up and just worshipped God and then it happened. His situation helped me realize one thing. It's not something you earn, it's a gift. It was a promised gift to me.

"He that believeth and is baptized shall be saved; but he that believeth not shall be damned." "And these signs shall follow them that believe; In my name shall they cast out devils; they shall speak with new tongues;"
Mark 16:16-17

After the guest was done speaking, the Pastor asked me, "Sister Shaunte' do you want to receive the Holy Ghost?" "Yes" "Well come up here. You're gonna get it."

Now? I'm about to get it now? Everything started to move in slow motion. My legs trembled in anticipation. The entire congregation had gathered at the front and a few other people came up to receive the Holy Ghost as well.

People had gathered around me like they were about to go into battle. I had a circle of saints all around me. Some had already started to lay hands on my back and shoulder.

One brother of the congregation told me the one thing that no one had ever explained to me. He had a bit of swag to him; it was more of a realness. Sometimes church people tended to be so surreal and perfect. It was like they lived in a perfect world where they walked on cotton-candy clouds with Jesus all day. But my life was nothing like that. I needed someone I could relate too, someone who wasn't so perfect or would front to be so.

The brother looked at me and said, "Hey man, now I know it's a lot of people around but they not paying attention to you. They're praying for you. So you just pray, don't worry about the people around you." And that's what I did.

Like the prophet had said a year ago, I lifted my hands and surrendered to God. I forgot about the people around me, closed my eyes and immediately I saw an image of Christ's head when he was on the cross.

He died for me. He died for *me*. He died so that I could have this moment. Being sealed until the day of redemption. I opened my mouth to say Hallelujah. But an unknown language came out. My spirit was filled. That void inside of me felt physically full. It was like a radiant light filled me and beamed out like a sunburst. I could not contain myself I started walking all around knocking people off of me. It was ok, they could let go now. God had filled me with His Spirit.

And the disciples were filled with joy, and with the Holy Ghost.
Acts 13:52

I was saved, sanctified, Holy Ghost filled and fire-baptized. The fire: that was the essential part. It took the fire of God to burn those things away that were not of Him and purify me to be used in the Kingdom.

I was a very zealous new born. I was teaching a home Bible Study to others 6 months after I got saved. It was too soon. But, my Pastor let me learn on my own because I was also a very sensitive Christian. I was easily hurt and offended. It's as if I was a burn victim, any little finger that touched me, I wailed in agony. I would soon learn that I had a lot of restorative work to be done.

I watched a documentary about a woman that had a tumor on her back the size of a beach ball. And I wondered why she let the tumor get to such a size before she sought help? It took them years to remove the tumor, because it had become such a part of the woman that removing the entire tumor at once could kill her. She had to have multiple surgeries in order for them to remove the tumor and salvage her life. As they removed pieces of the grotesque tumor they also found all types of weird things out of place like teeth and hair. Eventually the doctors were successful at removing the tumor but it took the woman years to heal and begin to walk "right" after surgery.

Traumatic things happened to me as a child but in my adulthood I brought in and even welcomed troubling things into my life. My soul had been saved but the consequences of my life of sin still plagued me. It had become apart of me. I was living a single, carefree life where premarital sex was acceptable and going out to the club on the weekends was my thing. And who could forget daily happy hours?

When I raised my hands and surrendered to God. I surrendered everything. I turned in ladies' night for Bible Study; Saturday parties for cleaning the church.

The process was gracious and many times painful. My flesh despised the purge; sometimes the spirit man won and sometimes the flesh. I was in disbelief of the boisterous tug-of-war. The devil fought hard against me. He even sent people to attack me inside the church. But God continued to renew me and show me a better way despite my fallings.

"Moreover the law entered, that the offence might abound. But where sin abounded, grace did much more abound:"
Romans 5:20

In 2009 the ladies at my church were attending a conference in Tennessee called the Esther Project. The night before God sent me a dream of my rape. It felt like it was happening all over again except for I had the consciousness of an adult. I was powerless, embarrassed and angrier now that I understood what was happening. It felt so real, I thought I would reach up and punch the woman in the face.

Then, God showed me a vision of a brain. There were traces of blood inside each of its wrinkles as if it had been pulled out of my head during a surgery. At the top of the brain, in the center, was a deep gash. It looked like someone had took an axe and chopped into it.

I woke up terrified. I jumped out of bed as if the woman from my dream was on top of me. I dropped to my knees in grief. I asked got with almost an attitude and anger, "Lord why? Why did you show me that?" I didn't want to visit that place. I hid that event so deep within me, it took God Himself to reach into the depths of my soul and pull it out.

On the way to Tennessee from St. Louis I talked to the ladies in the car about my dream in hopes of an interpretation. I had never told anyone of what happened to me. No one. Yet in desperation I reached out and made myself completely vulnerable. Sister Emily said, "Well, maybe that's why you're going to the conference. God is going to deal with this issue in your life." So there it was, I went to that conference with an expectancy of being healed and delivered.

During one of the general sessions of the conference a minister from Jamaica spoke. She talked about how the devil had attacked women sexually in the church and how it effects us in our daily lives unknowingly; married and single women. For married women, they were having intimacy issues with their husbands. The married women felt like intimacy was a dirty thing. They had a hard time being naked in front of their husbands because they had been violated. Single women were having issues with fear of becoming married or committing to celibacy until marriage. I immediately connected with the message.

She asked each woman that had been molested as a young girl to stand. Almost every woman in the room stood. "Find a sister around you. The two of you hold hands and face each other. Tell the sister what happened to you, how it made you feel and how it's affecting you now. Then, pray for her healing and she'll pray for yours."

"You have to allow time to heal, for God to heal you," the preacher said. "See, some of you are walking around with Band-Aids over these wounds. Those Band-Aids aren't helping a thing. We see that you're still hurt and bleeding. Some wounds need to be stitched. In the natural some wounds are so deep that they can't be stitched they have to be packed."

When a wound is deep, or when it tunnels under the skin, packing the wound can help it heal. The packing material absorbs any drainage from the wound, which helps the tissues heal from the inside out. Without the packing, the wound might close at the top, without healing at the deeper areas of the wound. (Nagy, 2013)

This was my issue. My wound from being raped had closed at the top. I looked like I had it all together. I had finally given my life to Christ. I was attempting to free myself of things that reminded me of my life or sin or coerced me back into it. But the deeper areas of my wound remained unhealed and infected. That sexually abusive moment implanted me with a poisonous perverted mindset.

No matter how hard I tried sex had been a stronghold in my life. I misused it unaware of its real purpose. I used it to solidify my relationships. I used it to get materialistic things that I wanted but could not acquire on my own. I used it as power to control a man to do every task I needed done. I used it to fix arguments and mask my mental flaws. I used it to forget about my troubles, relieve the stress of life and gain self-confidence.

By giving my life to Christ I gave up my personal "golden goose". It would be self-slandering to say that I didn't resent it. I wanted God to quickly replace what I gave up for Him. I expected to be married within a year. There was no way I would be able to resist something that had become such a great part of me.

Even though I had the Holy Ghost I still desired so much more. I needed to be healed. It seemed impossible. How was God not enough?

I turned to my sister and she turned to me. We shared things that were very deep, dark and debilitating. With tears and groans we went back to those places with God as our Redeemer, we were set free. The chains of perversion and abuse had been released from our hearts and minds.

I prayed and asked God to heal me, to heal me now. The sooner I was healed the sooner I could get married and not be inprisoned to the sexual temptation.

I got home from the conference two days later. I knelt at the side of my bed and asked God, "How? Lord how are you going to heal me, I get the rape and why you gave me the dream but what about my mind?"

Instantly God sent me vision. I saw the bloody brain again with the gash still in it from earlier. Even after I had prayed and asked for healing at the conference. Then, I saw a black book falling from heaven. The Book slid into the gash of my brain. On the spine of the book it read *Holy Bible.* "My Word," God said, "That's how I'm going to heal you. With My Word."

I started to cry and pray in the Holy Ghost. Thanking God for what He was about to do in my life. He was going to heal me.

I started to print out copies of the Word on strips of paper and taped them to the walls of my house. I had them in the closet, the bathroom, my bedroom, the kitchen, everywhere I spent the most time. There were lots of key scriptures from Hosea that I used. This book spoke to me distinctively. Particularly because I felt that during this time God had placed me in the wilderness in order to take me through the healing process.

"Therefore, behold, I will allure her, and bring her into the wilderness, and speak comfortably unto her."
Hosea 2:14

God started to purge me of things I held on to; my old way of thinking, living and even dressing. Until God stripped me of it, I didn't realize how mean I was to people. I felt like they owed me something. Because, I grew up so harshly and bullied by others I would be overtly mean to people; even the ones that didn't hurt me personally.

He started to strip me of my old defenses and persona. I used my achievements and organizational affiliations to gain the admiration of others, my outside adoration to gain the popularity and favor, intimidation to protect me from the offenses of others. God took those things from me and replaced it with His glory and favor on my life.

I found my beauty in Him. There were days that God would show me how beautiful I was to Him, the beauty of holiness and the glory of the inward man.

I spent years recovering from my old life. Around the third year after I was saved I made a few requests to God: *I want to be married but I don't want children.* I had started to teach in inner city St. Louis and I recognized the behaviors of my younger self in many of the students I taught. I became aware of the abusive cases in our school. I just couldn't bear doing that to one of my children. How could I be sure that I wouldn't perpetuate the cycle?

God answered by letting me know, that that wasn't truly what I wanted. He showed me the contents of my heart. Which cried out the opposite of what my mouth had requested. I started to have dreams of children, my children. I started to dream of my husband.

I thought God was punishing me by showing me things I didn't have and would probably never have. I was starting to fall into that "I'm not good enough" rut.

God sent me a vision. A vision of Cinderella when the Prince came to her house and put the glass slipper on her foot.

When the Prince saw Cinderella for the first time she wore the most beautiful dress ever made, a diamond tiara and glass slippers. Her hair was perfect and her make up was flawless. She left abruptly at 11:59 leaving behind a remarkable glass slipper. She left behind a luxury item and didn't come back for it. Surely, she comes from a wealthy family that lavishes her in expensive gifts.

The Prince arrived at her house, tried the shoe on her stepsisters and even the mother. When Cinderella was finally called for, she came around the corner with her head down in shame. She wore ragged clothes and she had no shoes. The apron and the handkerchief were the sure indicators that she was nothing more but a mistreated servant. Yet, he called her over to him so that he could put the glass slipper on her foot. He saw the truth about her. He knew her condition but he still loved her. He searched all over for her and she had a place in his kingdom.

But God commendeth his love toward us, in that, while we were yet sinners, Christ died for us.
Romans 5:8

God was there the entire time. He knew my past and me. All of things I had done to myself. All of the things that were done to me. My righteousness was as filthy rags. Yet He had a place for me in His kingdom.

I would spend several days locked in my apartment fasting, praying and allowing God to heal me. The most profound exercise God had me do was to right down all of the things that had happened to me that made me not want a family of my own. I placed them all in a bag and one by one I would tell God descriptively what happened and after I would forgive. I would have to forgive three people: the trespasser, my self and God. Not that God needed forgiveness but sometimes I would tend to hold something against God that was caused by my sin and others. I should not have held back from God, the One that would deliver.

I would pray and say, "Lord I forgive ______. Please lay not this sin to their charge. I do not want them to be punished for this wrong. Lord I forgive myself. I will not hold myself back by dwelling on that situation and punishing myself. Lord you were there when all of these things happened to me and You allowed it to happen. I do not hold that against you. I release it unto you."

During this time period God told me that I had some things in me. Things that if I didn't allow Him to take out of me, I wasn't going to be a good wife or mother. *So it's true*, I thought, *one day I will be married and be a mom.*

I yielded to the process. It was long and hard and I wanted to give up. I persevered because I wanted the very best. I had come to far to give up and settle for being a half-healed, needy and broken woman.

By the time God was done with me I was fine with being single the rest of my life. But that wasn't the plan. The plan was for me to become someone's helpmeet, a nurturing and caring wife. The plan was for me to become someone's praying mother, a mother to teach them the word of God.

My husband had surely obtained favor from the Lord. I was a praying, fasting, soul-winning machine. God taught me how to forgive, how to love, how to be submissive, how to not be contentious.

In 2012 I completed my student teaching at a high school in St. Louis. It had always been my dream to carry on the profession like my favorite teacher Mrs. Austin. I was walking around the school so happy and whole. I was healed of my issues and God had allowed me to complete a second Master's degree in education. While greeting the school secretary I noticed a guy in uniform staring at me and smiling from a far. My first thought was: *back up and don't look this way. I'm not looking for a man.*

The school secretary felt so obliged to introduce us. I told him about how I had a recruiter in high school as well, just small talk. But this guy was just staring like he was interested in getting to know me personally, not just as one of the teachers. So I quickly ended the conversation and went about my way.

Two weeks later I was approached by the school's Career Counselor, she had a good friend of the family that had met me recently. She went on to say that he had been asking her, for the past two weeks, about Miss Anderson. I was so flattered but honestly I couldn't remember meeting anyone.

A few days later he came to visit me at the school. As soon as I saw him I thought, "Lord Jesus, who is this?" He was so handsome, tall, in great shape and he was a Marine. I had never met a black marine before. He was a perfect gentleman, he never called me late at night or stared at my booty…I had to go home and pray about this before I got too excited, because it could be just another counterfeit.

Soon after, I started to get several confirmations that Chris was the one. He was everything I had prayed for. We were married less than year later.

When we tell the story of how we met my husband's story always gives me butterflies. He says: "I was talking to the registrar, getting transcripts and I saw her walk by me. And I said, 'Who is that'? Ms. Russell said, 'Oh that's Miss Anderson. Ms. Russell called her over and my eyes were just fixated on her. She had on a pink ruffled shirt and a looong black skirt. And I knew that was her."

Just like that, he had found me. I spent all of those years being healed, but crying and begging at the same time for a man that I wasn't ready for. But when the time was right God sent him. He sent him to find me. It wasn't my hair, my clothes, my body or what I had to offer. The glory of God on my life, led him to his wife.

When it was all said and done. I was glad it took me four years of being single and enduring the process. I was broken, abused and misused, but God. HE healed me. HE changed me. HE accepted me. HE loved me. HE died for me. HE is my first and true love. HE gets all the glory, then, now and forever more.

References

ARMY.MIL Features. (n.d.). Retrieved December 9, 2014, from http://www.army.mil/values/

Inception [Motion picture on DVD]. (2010). Warner Bros. Entertainment, Inc. :.

Nagy, K. (2013, August 1). Discharge Instructions for Wound Cares. Retrieved December 9, 2014, from http://www.aast.org/discharge-instructions-for-wound-cares

www.ingramcontent.com/pod-product-compliance
Ingram Content Group UK Ltd.
Pitfield, Milton Keynes, MK11 3LW, UK
UKHW020128250726
13967UKWH00002B/528

9 781312 672529